Against Austerity

DUE

D0732575

Against Austerity

How We Can Fix the Crisis They Made

Richard Seymour

www.plutobooks.com

First published 2014 by Pluto Press
345 Archway Road, London N6 5AA

www.plutobooks.com

Distributed in the United States of America exclusively by
Palgrave Macmillan, a division of St. Martin's Press LLC,
175 Fifth Avenue, New York, NY 10010

British Library Cataloguing in Publication Data
A catalogue record for this book is available from the British Library

ISBN   978 0 7453 3329 8   Hardback
ISBN   978 0 7453 3328 1   Paperback
ISBN   978 1 7837 1019 5   PDF eBook
ISBN   978 1 7837 1021 8   Kindle eBook
ISBN   978 1 7837 1020 1   EPUB eBook

Library of Congress Cataloging in Publication Data applied for

This book is printed on paper suitable for recycling and made from
fully managed and sustained forest sources. Logging, pulping and
manufacturing processes are expected to conform to the environmental
standards of the country of origin.

10   9   8   7   6   5   4   3   2   1

Typeset from disk by Stanford DTP Services, Northampton, England
Text design by Melanie Patrick
Simultaneously printed digitally by CPI Antony Rowe, Chippenham, UK and
Edwards Bros in the United States of America

Contents

Preface

If the case for austerity was an email, it would be the rough equivalent of one of those badly spelled inducements to join an organ trafficking ring or give your bank details to a penis enlargement specialist. Most people would have figuratively clicked 'delete' and moved on to some other specimen of the exhausted culture of late capitalism – a veritable lolocaust. But the rulers of the world aren't so easy to ignore. Their resources are infinitely more sophisticated than spammers, their appeals are insidiously effective, as are the false cues and misdirection.

I hope this book can be useful in disentangling some of this. Each chapter does indeed attempt to unfold the real processes behind the convenient label, 'austerity'. However, it shouldn't be seen as one of the many volumes debunking austerity. The crucial problem which this book addresses is that the current opponents of austerity – primarily Left and labour movements – are in the main poorly placed to stop it, or even significantly impede it. How can it be, for example, that we have come this far without – figuratively, of course – ornamenting the major financial centres with the entrails and severed heads of bankers? I said, figuratively. And how is it that, far from expunging this swarm of parasites, we are *more dependent on them than ever before*? Doesn't such dependency make a mockery of the term 'parasite'?

I think our analysis of what austerity is, how it works, and what strategies can best stop it, has been badly wrong. But it is not simply a question of flawed perspectives – this is merely symptomatic. There are a range of political styles on the Left, a set of discursive habits, and models of organisation, which were inherited from past failure. These need to be broken with. This is not a cause for resignation, but for reviewing and rethinking. It is a cause for breaking with consolatory ideology and convenient forgetting. Understanding the problem is an essential part of overcoming it.

I should warn the reader to expect a certain sneering negativity to very occasionally peep through in this book. That is because, well, I'm frankly a bit fucked off about all this. Like practically everyone else on the Left, I expected to be able to meet the worst crisis of capitalism in generations with more aplomb than has hitherto been evident. Particularly when our opponents are, as Glen Cullen put it in *The Thick of It*, a bunch of 'six-toed, born-to-rule ponyfuckers'.

But this is good news. Gramsci said that he didn't like to throw stones in the dark. He needed something to oppose in order to stimulate his thinking about situations, historical controversies, philosophical problems, or political struggles. The advantage of writing a polemical book like this is that there is no danger of throwing stones in the dark. Highly visible targets are everywhere: and as Daphne and Celeste would put it, they ain't got no alibi.

There is also a certain familiar use of esoteric political theory and rococo ornamentation that some readers will find off-putting. I hope so anyway. Those readers would be far better off reading something else. (Or, alternatively, stay and have your middlebrow sensibilities challenged.) This book comes with swearing and unapologetic intellectual swagger.

I imagine you're scanning this page while still in the bookshop, calculating whether you'd be willing to be seen reading this book on the train. If the above appeals to you, you're probably a bit 'wrong' in some way, but I welcome you. If it doesn't, then make your way to the holy apotheosis of bookshops that is the '3 for 2' section. And buy yet more inconsequential shit with which to line your shelf of good intentions.

Acknowledgements

This book was written with indecent haste and mainly involved solidifying thoughts and ideas that had been developing for some time. But even in that short time, a number of friends provided references, feedback and (goddamn them) criticism. For example, I road-tested some of these ideas in front of a room full of American friends and comrades, who had the good sense to disagree with almost all of them.

China Miéville and Rosie Warren provided invaluable, sarcy comments on the drafts – huge thanks to them. Thanks also to Sebastian Budgen for an almost daily supply of references, many of which ended up in this book. And above all, thanks to the editor at Pluto Press, David Shulman, who offered kindly and intelligent guidance, and made me take out the jokes that didn't work.

Introduction:
The Bad News Gospel

The crisis creates situations which are dangerous in the short run, since the various strata of the population are not all capable of orienting themselves equally swiftly, or of reorganizing with the same rhythm. The traditional ruling class, which has numerous trained cadres, changes men and programmes and, with greater speed than is achieved by subordinate classes, reabsorbs the control that was slipping from its grasp. Perhaps it may make sacrifices, and expose itself to an uncertain future by demagogic promises; but it retains power, reinforces it for the time being, and uses it to crush its adversary and disperse his leading cadres, who cannot be very numerous or highly trained. – *Antonio Gramsci*.[1]

Rather than witnessing a shift in the balance of class forces toward workers and popular movements, the course of the crisis has favored the capitalist class. – *Greg Albo, Sam Gindin and Leo Panitch*[2]

Five Years of Glorious Failure

The fifth anniversary of the collapse of Lehman Brothers will have passed before this book is published. If, between now and then, the Left has got its shit together, this book will make a nice gift for someone you don't like. In the more probable scenario that it hasn't, I invite the reader to linger on this salient fact. A week is an

---

1. Antonio Gramsci, 'State and Civil Society', in Quintin Hoare and Geoffrey Nowell Smith, eds., *Selections from the Prison Notebooks of Antonio Gramsci*, Lawrence & Wishart, London, 1971, pp. 210–11.
2. Greg Albo, Sam Gindin and Leo Panitch, *In and Out of Crisis: The Global Financial Meltdown and Left Alternatives*, PM Press, Oakland, CA, 2010, p. 37.

eternity in politics. Five years of crisis with nothing to show for it is jaw dropping, particularly when set against what might have been expected. This book is thus about a historical missed opportunity, a failure. It accentuates the negative. It is 'pessimistic'. Deal with it.

It is not just the practical irrelevance of most of the Left's actions to date that have to be audited, but also the outstanding success (to date) of what is called 'austerity'. This will immediately raise the heckles of those on the Left who argue that austerity is a calamitous failure. But that claim is based on a misunderstanding of what austerity is.

Admittedly, the label 'austerity' covers a multitude of sins. For parts of the Right, the argument is simple. You can't spend more than you take in; sound finances means clearing debts as quickly as possible. In this version of events, the state is something like a household, and austerity nothing more than a little belt-tightening. For the Left, which knows that the state is nothing like a household, it looks like a simple bait and switch job, transferring the costs of a crisis of the banks onto the public sector, thus harming working people and protecting the rich.

But that is to reduce austerity to spending cuts, when what is going on is a lot broader and more complex. To grasp this, it is necessary to distinguish austerity from the general constraints on spending imposed under neoliberalism – as institutionalised, for example, in the EU Stability and Growth Pact, which limits borrowing and deficits. The latter could be called 'austerity lite' or 'permanent austerity', but it really doesn't have the same political function as the kinds of austerity programmes I will discuss in this book. For example, Obama's spending cuts are characteristic of his fiscal conservatism and acceptance of basic neoliberal orthodoxy, but they are far removed from the kinds of austerity programmes implemented by Republican governors. And the latter go far beyond spending cuts.

Take the policies implemented under austerity in the United Kingdom. Whether it is cuts to the minimum wage, the introduction of private provision in the National Health Service and schools, or changes in the tax structure to benefit the wealthy, these are policies whose overall thrust is unlikely to increase revenues to the Treasury. In fact, as regards the changes to public services, the involvement of private companies such as Virgin, as well as the wasteful 'markets' imposed on providers, will probably drive up costs and lead to further fiscal crises. No one is suggesting that the state will stop collecting the taxes to fund core services such as pensions, healthcare and education. And even if they are under-funded, and the provision is rationed in ways that favour residents of relatively wealthy, middle-class areas, it is highly unlikely that the tendency for costs to increase will subside.

Services and benefits can be pared down, and cost-suppressing measures implemented. But there is reason to doubt that the British state will cost much less in ten years' time, as a proportion of GDP, than it has over the preceding twenty years. In the period from 1987 to 2007, during which there was only one recession of medium severity, public spending was generally kept at or below 40 per cent of GDP, a feat last accomplished during the high growth years of the 1950s. In a period of sustained crisis, this becomes extremely difficult not only because growth is depressed and social overheads are inflated, but because the costs of investment relative to profits are higher, and capital constantly needs incentives from the state to put its money into circulation. Even once the crisis recedes and a period of relative capitalist dynamism resumes, this particular neoliberal format of capitalist dependency on the state will continue to drive up costs.

What we are witnessing, under the auspices of austerity, is not simply spending cuts. It is a shift in the entire civilisational edifice of capitalism, deepening an equivalent shift that began in the mid 1970s. These processes include:

1) A drastic, long-term 'rebalancing' of economies away from consumption and toward investment – that is, away from wages and toward profits.
2) The growing strength of financial capital within capitalist economies and the accompanying spread of 'precarity' in all areas of life.
3) The recomposition of social classes, with more inequality and more stratification within classes.

4) The growing penetration of the state by corporations.[3]
5) The reorganisation of the state as a less welfarist and more penal and coercive institution.
6) Accompanying it all, the dissemination of cultures which value hierarchy, competitiveness and casual sadism toward the weak.

Not all of these processes are under the control of national states, but states do anticipate, organise and promote them in crucial ways. It is in this respect that the term 'austerity' has some uses here: it gives a political name to these processes and identifies the dominant role of politics in their formation.

This is important, because austerity is justified primarily as an *economic* strategy, in response to an economic crisis. We pay off the debt, capitalists gain confidence in the likely future condition of the economy and start to invest – growth and employment ensues. However, if austerity was just an attempt to deal with an economic crisis in *this* sense, it would have been terminated already. It would have failed.

But a crisis of capitalism is not just an economic crisis. Inevitably, since the state is so profoundly involved in the organisation of the economy, and since it chose to exercise its clout by guaranteeing a privatised banking system against failure, it became a *political* crisis. But it also – as the ensuing recession accentuated a crisis of profitability for the newspapers, undermined faith in parliament and the established parties, and intersected in the UK with a long-developing scandal involving the Murdoch press, the dominant political parties and the police – became an *ideological* crisis.

Here it might be useful to apply Gramsci's term 'organic crisis', to refer to a *general impasse* of society and state, not merely of the capitalist market. Certainly, it begins with acute economic dysfunction, but it is rapidly overdetermined by multiple other breakdowns. It eventually constitutes a crisis of authority, of the dominant political and cultural institutions, of the forms of consent

---

3. A process the journalist George Monbiot captured vividly, with scrupulous and outraged reporting, at the beginning of the New Labour era. See his *Captive State: The Corporate Takeover of Britain*, Pan Books, London, 2001.

and coercion. It results in unpredictable breakdowns at various levels and outbreaks of insubordination by heterogeneous social groups – students, women, precarious workers, trade unionists, young people and so on.

Gramsci insisted that in such a situation the 'traditional ruling class' is at a considerable advantage over opponents, because of its existing power. Its control over the dominant institutions, its loyal cadres of supporters in think-tanks and the media, its economic and political strength, all enable it to adapt better to the crisis and propose solutions which meet its interests. Proactively, it seeks to meet the crisis on every level on which it manifests itself by changing strategies, winning over popular layers with 'demagogic promises', and preempting and isolating opponents. This is a conception of crisis as a moment of urgent, bitterly contested struggle, rather than as simply something akin to a natural catastrophe or an act of the gods.

The austerity project, seen in this light, is not just a matter of good husbandry, but neither is it simply a short-sighted attempt by the rich to shirk the costs of economic failure. Rather, it is a multi-dimensional response to crisis. In the short term, as a tactical response, it preempts opponents by providing an explanation for the crisis – high levels of public and private debt, lack of competitiveness – which resonates with elements of common experience and which is connotatively linked to its proposed solutions. While oppositional forces slowly and warily begin to formulate an analysis, some objectives, some strategies and tactics, those advancing the austerity project have already begun the battle in the chambers of commerce, the business and parliamentary lobbies, the newspapers, and so on. By the time a demand is articulated – nationalise the banks!, tax the rich! – the austerians have already subtly shifted the agenda and perspective. Yes, they concede the point about irresponsible financiers, who must be 'regulated', but they are far more concerned about the feckless poor suckling off the welfare teat, maxing out their credit cards, and draining the productive layers of society. Remove this irresponsible burden, let the wealth creators create, and the good old days will return.

This tactical success would be of no use, however, if it was not linked to a long-term, strategic response to crisis, which recognises that things must change drastically if they are to stay the same. In this sense, austerity is an attempt to shift the material foundations of society in a fashion which partially addresses the causes of crisis, but which does so on terms compatible with the interests of the 'traditional ruling class'. And it is at the level of *politics*, not economics, that this response is organised.

If much of the Left has been slow to respond to the crisis, it has been because it either misunderstood the politics involved, assuming that bailouts equalled the end of neoliberalism, or it expected something else more akin to a 'classic' economic crisis with mass unemployment and wage cuts resulting in strikes and flying pickets. Since both of these positions have proven to be inadequate, it is necessary to re-examine some founding assumptions.

Austerity, Bailouts and Neoliberalism

One of the most widespread notions after the credit crunch began was the belief that neoliberalism had collapsed. On both the Left and the Right, nothing was more certain. The US government, under the lame duck Bush administration, was engaged in activism on a scale unseen since FDR. There were nationalisations and untold billions of public money invested in bailouts for financial institutions. This looked a great deal like the right-wing vision of 'socialism'.

The BBC journalist Paul Mason, in one of the first detailed books on the crisis and the global institutional response, exhorted his readers to realise that neoliberalism 'is over: as an ideology, as an economic model. Get used to it and move on.'[4] The choice, he insisted, was between the immediate nationalisation of the banks and a massive public works programme, implying a greatly expanded productivist state, or a prolonged global slump. The rich texture of Mason's analysis and reportage, displaying his unusual critical intelligence, makes it doubly compelling that he was so wrong. The

---

4. Paul Mason, *Meltdown: The End of the Age of Greed*, Verso, London and New York, 2009.

principal reason why he and others were wrong is because they reduced neoliberalism to 'free market fundamentalism'. The national state's emergence as a major factor in the global economy seemed to spell the end of such 'free market' ideologies, and allowed people to imagine that the end of the neoliberal era was afoot.

Others such as David Harvey were more realistic in allowing that the type of neoliberalism that dominated government was a 'pragmatic neoliberalism', distinct from the popular 'free market' justifications. In this version, bailing out the banks was the permitted exception to the liberalising, free market writ. Moreover, Harvey correctly anticipated that the ruling class might actually prefer to retreat behind the fortress walls and accept a period of global slump rather than support the implementation of an agenda of public spending and demand management that could strengthen unions and significantly reduce the political power of investors.[5] Nonetheless, this overall perspective accepts too much of the idea that what neoliberals are interested in is a minimal, 'night watchman' state. This is *not* how neoliberals see the state.

Neoliberalism is not a simple reiteration of the principles of classical liberalism – a defence of the 'market society'. It has its origins in an authoritarian reconfiguration of liberalism, beginning in the early twentieth century, specifically designed to meet the challenge of mass democracy and the welfarist demands that came with it.[6] The great pioneer of this shift was Friedrich Hayek, subsequently the *éminence grise* of what the economist Philip Mirowski dubs the 'Neoliberal Thought Collective', and a great influence on Mrs Thatcher.

---

5. See David Harvey, *A Brief History of Neoliberalism*, Oxford University Press, Oxford, 2005; David Harvey, *The Enigma of Capital And the Crisis of Capitalism*, Profile Books, London, 2010.

6. I describe aspects of this in *The Meaning of David Cameron*, Zero Books, Winchester, 2010, pp. 32–4. See also William E. Scheuerman, *Carl Schmitt: The End of Law*, Rowman & Littlefield, Lanham MD, 1999; Renato Christi, *Carl Schmitt and Authoritarian Liberalism: Strong State, Free Economy*, University of Wales Press, Cardiff, 1998; and Philip Mirowski, *Never Let a Serious Crisis Go To Waste: How Neoliberalism Survived the Financial Meltdown*, Verso, London and New York, 2013.

Hayek obscured his real sympathies regarding the state with talk of the 'spontaneous order' of the market. But it is clear that he thought a very strong state necessary for various reasons. One such was to cope with the pathologies of democracy, which lent itself to collectivism and welfarism. The modern democratic state allowed workers to become politically active and to demand the protection of their interests and some attempt at 'planning' the economy in accord with a general interest in full employment, growth and so on. Through monopolistic organisations such as trade unions workers were able to flex political muscle in the pursuit of these ends. For Hayek, no general interest existed – or at least, it was impossible to calculate such a general interest. All that welfare institutions accomplished was the distortion of the universality of the 'rule of law' by making it serve particular interests. By entangling the sovereign state in a mesh of claims and counter-claims, demands for intervention, demands for help, mass democracy had weakened the state.

In his later writings – particularly *Law, Legislation and Liberty* – the attempt to contain democracy became a far more explicit aspect of Hayek's agenda. Intriguingly, Hayek scholars tend to agree that his authoritarian liberalism owed far more to the Nazi legal scholar Carl Schmitt than he was willing to admit. His critique of the welfare state in particular was strikingly close to Schmitt's critique of the party political state. None of this is to say that Hayek outright opposed democracy. He felt it had certain provisional advantages. It was a source of political legitimacy and stability, and if properly handled it could gradually teach a population to abhor socialism.[7] Nonetheless, his comment on the Pinochet regime in 1981 – that he preferred a liberal dictatorship to a democracy lacking all liberalism – characteristically expressed his order of preferences.

As a rule, neoliberals maintain a strict distinction between liberalism and democracy. A liberal society may be democratic or authoritarian: provided it safeguards 'liberty', it remains a liberal

---

7. See Perry Anderson, 'The Intransigent Right', in *Spectrum: From Left to Right in the World of Ideas*, Verso, London and New York, 2005, p. 16; also Friedrich Hayek, *The Constitution of Liberty*, University of Chicago Press, Chicago, IL, 1960, Chapter 7.

society. Clearly, the 'liberty' upheld by the Mont Pelerin Society, a central institutional component in the multiplex of neoliberal institutions, is not *political* liberty. It is not the liberty to participate in the politics of a society. It is the liberty to engage in market transactions, to buy and sell on terms set by 'the market'. It is the liberty to be at the mercy of 'the blind force of social process', as Hayek put it.[8]

Yet this 'blind force' is only apparent. The phrase implies that the economy is akin to a natural system, driven by brutal, merciless physical laws. And indeed, there is a tendency in neoliberal ideology to explain 'the market' as a pitiless evolutionary system, weeding out the weak and inadequate through competition and selection.[9]

However, as Michel Foucault pointed out in his late '70s lectures on neoliberalism, neoliberals don't really believe in such 'spontaneous order'. Rather, they firmly believe that the market system has to be fixed in place by a legal regime, which is the contingent product of human action. A neoliberal legal order is thus one that regulates the economy quite extensively, but it specifically forecloses the possibility of any kind of economic plan. Since the general good is not calculable, and since the state cannot attain a general knowledge of the economy, it must not seek a particular purpose but only regulate by introducing formal, general maxims.

Moreover, since neoliberals recognise that human beings are not necessarily predisposed to embrace 'the market', the law must not only protect the market order from popular attempts to subordinate it, but also help create neoliberal subjects. People must be compelled to embrace their 'entrepreneurial' selves, to treat every aspect of their lives as a self-maximising quest, and to embrace the calculus of risks and rewards in the market, including the inequalities that come with it, rather than seeking to control it. Attempts at circumventing or

---

8. Quoted in Mirowski, *Never Let a Serious Crisis Go To Waste*, p. 84.

9. See Philip Mirowski, 'On the Origins (at Chicago) of some Species of Neoliberal Evolutionary Economics', in Robert van Horn, Philip Mirowski and Thomas A. Stapleford, eds., *Building Chicago Economics: New Perspectives on the History of America's Most Powerful Economics Program*, Cambridge University Press, Cambridge, 2011.

subverting the economic order, whether through political activism or criminality, must be harshly punished. The neoliberal state is a big,[10] interventionist state, particularly in its penal mode.[11]

Not merely big and authoritarian, the neoliberal state is increasingly penetrated by private sector companies. Hayek, following Schmitt, had argued that social democracy compromised the state's autonomy, by enmeshing it in a web of interests and client relationships. Later neoliberals further theorised this conception, arguing that public sector bureaucrats, far from being driven by a 'public service' ethic, are just self-maximising 'entrepreneurs', like any actor in the market. From Anthony Downs' famous 'economic' conception of democracy, to the 'public choice' economics of John Buchanan and William Niskanen, this analysis allowed neoliberals to argue that state bureaucrats are incentivised by democracy to raise their own budgets, increase staff count, and serve special interests. They argued that this inflated the costs of the state and distorted its general functioning, and that the only effective response was to openly acknowledge the self-interested behaviour of bureaucrats and use it to incentivise efficiency and industry. This meant simulating 'market' mechanisms, with internal competition and budget caps, and bringing in 'experts' from business to push through reforms.

Increasingly, because it was assumed that businessmen were the real experts at running things, it also meant taking decisions out of the hands of elected representatives – so sensitive to special interests – and putting them in the hands of unelected bodies populated by corporate managers and technocrats, or outsourcing them to private firms, or engaging companies in various lucrative 'partnerships'. The result of all this is not a shrinking state, but a state in which there is a growing internal articulation of the dominance of large

---

10. 'Big', not just in terms of its overall cost, but also in terms of the wide-ranging scope of its involvement in organising daily life.

11. See Michel Foucault, *The Birth of Biopolitics: Lectures at the College de France, 1978–1979*, Palgrave Macmillan, Basingstoke, 2008; also, Mirowski, *Never Let a Serious Crisis Go To Waste*; and Loïc Wacquant, *Punishing the Poor: The Neoliberal Government of Social Insecurity*, Duke University Press, Durham, NC, 2009.

corporations. It doesn't mean that that 'markets' are 'freed' from state intervention; it means that the state is *ever more involved* in organising corporate dominance.

It is worth adding that, to help enforce the appropriate legal regime, neoliberals believe in the necessity of disciplined, cabal-like political organisation. The nexus of institutions, clubs and sodalities connecting neoliberals in different fields resembles nothing so much as the 'Russian doll' nightmare of 'Leninism' against which neoliberals pitched themselves during the Cold War.[12] This is not to say that neoliberal politics or the economic transformations that it helps organise can be reduced to the action of a tiny clique. It is simply to point to another of the ambiguities in neoliberal ideology – what Mirowski refers to as 'double truths' – in which the exoteric doctrine of 'spontaneous order' is falsified by the internal idiom and practice of neoliberals.

In short: the endless papers, newspaper articles and spiels about ending the nanny state and unleashing the market are calculated mythologies, which bear little relation to the esoteric doctrines that neoliberals actually share among themselves and with trusted audiences. The fact that the state has not significantly diminished in size during the neoliberal years, despite a significant assault on welfare, and that it has been consistently central to 'bailing out' neoliberal capitalism, should act as a warning sign here. It also gives us good grounds for reappraising what has happened in the last few years.

To take three major factors:

1) *Regulation.* A common demand on the liberal-left has been for the more effective regulation of the banks. This assumes that a *lack of regulation* was responsible for the financial system's collapse. Forms of deregulation did take place in the neoliberal era, chiefly to remove legal obstacles to financial dynamism. Yet, the result was not an under-regulated financial system. It was a system in which regulations were designed to enable speculative fever. In fact, as critics of this notion argue, 'freer markets often require more rules' to clarify the terms under which wildly varying trades take place, when

---

12. On this, see Mirowski, *Never Let a Serious Crisis Go To Waste*, Chapter 1.

property-owners' rights have been violated, when people can sue, and so on. This is particularly true if one thinks of the proliferation of new financial products and innovative debt mechanisms over the years. Certainly, regulation can be used to curtail fraud, protect consumers, or suppress profit-making excesses. But 'regulatory agencies weren't interested in that. Their role was developing the kinds of regulations that would promote financial innovation.'[13] The reality is that, strictly in terms of the numbers of laws and statutes on the books, Wall Street was more regulated after the abolition of the Glass-Steagall Act, which did constrain some abuses, than any market in history.[14] *Neoliberal capitalism is a highly regulated system.*

2) *Globalisation.* A mainstay of the neoliberal era has been the waning of the national state in the face of globalising commercial, financial and production trends. If companies can outsource production, move it abroad, or base their head office in a tax haven, or withdraw capital at a moment's notice, then state regulation, taxation and other controls seem fairly exiguous. These processes are very real, and have significant implications for the organisation of national states, which will be discussed in later chapters. For now I just want to underline that globalisation does not equal the decline of the nation-state. Research by Ruigrok and Tulder showed that, at the height of the neoliberal boom, at least 20 of the Fortune 100 top companies would not have still existed had they not been saved by their respective 'home' states, while many had benefited enormously from 'preferential defence contracts' and so on. Further, as Ellen Wood points out, citing the research of Alan Rutger, 'Scrutiny of corporate operations is likely to reveal that "multinational enterprises are not particularly good at managing their international operations", and that profits tend to be lower, while costs are higher, than in domestic

---

13. Albo, Gindin and Panitch, *In and Out of Crisis*, p. 35.
14. Leo Panitch and Martijn Konings, 'Myths of Neoliberal Deregulation', *New Left Review* 57, May–June 2009.

operations.'[15] What globalisation did was not diminish the state, but *internationalise* it. As such, it is no surprise at all that the national state has played such a prominent role in this crisis, and that *it has acted to protect globalisation.*

3) *Bailouts.* The scale of state 'intervention' in the years since 2007 has been colossal. Governments worldwide have infused trillions into the banks. The total federal assistance to banks in the US as of 2011 was over $29 trillion.[16] Many banks were ostensibly taken into public ownership. (They continued to operate, however, as commercial providers with considerable autonomy from the government. What we have seen is 'not so much the nationalization of the banks, but the privatization of the Treasury'.[17]) In themselves, extensive government bailouts are nothing new in the neoliberal era. Equivalent bailouts in US history include the rescue of New York City's finances during its fiscal crisis in the mid 1970s ($9.4 billion in 2008 currency), the 1980 bailout of Chrysler ($4 billion), the 1989 bailout of Savings and Loans ($293.3 billion), and the 2001 bailout of the airline industry ($18.6 billion). Hugely expensive bailouts took place in 1997 when the 'Asian tigers' went into crisis. Korea's bank bailout was equivalent to 31 per cent of GDP, Thailand's equivalent to 44 per cent, and

---

15. Ellen Meiksins Wood, *Empire of Capital*, Verso, London and New York, 2002, pp. 139–40; Ruigrok and Tulder cited in Chris Harman, 'Analysing Imperialism', *International Socialism* 2:99, Summer 2003, p. 43; Graeme Gill remarks that 'The forces of globalization themselves rely directly upon the state for their ability to function. Markets, NGOs, media companies and all the other institutions that propel globalization need to have some guarantees that they will not be subject to criminal or terrorist attack.' Graeme Gill, *The Nature and Development of the Modern State*, Palgrave Macmillan, Basingstoke, 2003, p. 248.

16. James Felkerson, '$29,000,000,000,000: A Detailed Look at the Fed's Bailout by Funding Facility and Recipient', Levy Economics Institute of Bard College, Working Paper No. 968, December 2011.

17. Julie Froud, Michael Moran, Adriana Nilsson, Karel Williams, 'Wasting a Crisis? Democracy and Markets in Britain After 2007,' *Political Quarterly* 81:1, 2010, pp. 25–38.

Indonesia's to 57 per cent.[18] Such state interventions are a routine feature of neoliberalism. Indeed, *they are usually part of the means by which neoliberalism is advanced.*

This is amply demonstrated in the first of several examples I will deal with in this book – the case of the New York City bailout.

Example 1: The Austerity State

The standard of living of the average American has to decline.[19]
– Paul Volcker

The collusion between neoliberalism and the *exceptional state*, whether it is a dictatorship or some other type of emergency regime, has once again come to the fore. In Greece and Italy particularly, emergency regimes – usually described as 'technocratic', simply because there is no significant elite opposition to their goals – have been imposed in order to sort out fiscal crises. In this way, neoliberal reforms have been introduced without the inconvenience of having to find a democratic mandate for them. Naomi Klein has identified this affinity as a core element of the 'shock doctrine', according to which crises are an opportunity to introduce deep structural changes that favour corporations and are extremely difficult to reverse.

From 1975 to 1978, New York City was subject to an austerity regime. This involved not simply a set of policies, but a temporary government – a set of special institutions with extraordinary, wide-ranging legal powers, the most important of which was the Emergency Financial Control Board (EFCB). The municipal corporation which ran the city cost $13 billion a year, but was in serious deficit. The EFCB, in conjunction with a number of other special institutions, responded by cutting services to low-income New Yorkers, attacking working

18. Figures from Jesse Nankin and Krista Kjellman Schmidt, 'History of US Gov't Bailouts', *Propublica*, 15 April 2009; and Matthew O'Brien, 'The Biggest Bank Bailouts in History', *The Atlantic*, 3 December 2012.
19. Quoted in Steven Rattner, 'Volcker Asserts US Must Trim Living Standard', *New York Times*, 17 October 1989. Note that Volcker was not expressing a Reaganite nostrum. This was also the view of the Carter White House.

conditions for the city's unionised workers, and offering incentives to its wealthy financial class.[20]

This experiment floated a set of policies designed to overcome deep-seated problems in the Fordist industries that had dominated since World War II, including declining profitability and competitiveness. The attempt to roll back state protections was linked to financialisation and the deregulation of markets, and the emergence of international dollar supremacy out of the collapse of Bretton-Woods. These solutions were already being road-tested outside the United States. Following the US-supported overthrow of the leftist Salvador Allende government in Chile, 1973, a team of economists trained in a Cold War programme to counteract leftism in Latin America were sent to help implement neoliberal ideas. As David Harvey describes the Chilean experiment:

> Working alongside the IMF, they restructured the economy according to their theories. They reversed the nationalizations and privatized public assets, opened up natural resources (fisheries, timber, etc.) to private and unregulated exploitation (in many cases riding roughshod over the claims of indigenous inhabitants), privatized social security, and facilitated foreign direct investment and freer trade. The right of foreign companies to repatriate profits from their Chilean operations was guaranteed. Export-led growth was favored over import substitution. The only sector reserved for the state was the key resource of copper (rather like oil in Iraq). This proved crucial to the budgetary viability of the state since copper revenues flowed exclusively into its coffers. The immediate revival of the Chilean economy in terms of growth rates, capital

---

20. This entire segment draws heavily on the analyses of three books in particular: Robert W. Bailey, *The Crisis Regime: The Mac, the ECFB, and the Political Impact of the New York City Financial Crisis*, State University of New York Press, New York, 1984; William K. Tabb, *The Long Default: New York City and the Urban Fiscal Crisis*, Monthly Review Press, New York, 1982; and by far the most important authority used throughout this discussion, Eric Lichten, *Class, Power and Austerity: The New York City Financial Crisis*, Bergin & Garvey Publishers Inc., Westport, CT, 1986.

accumulation, and high rates of return on foreign investments was short-lived. It all went sour in the Latin American debt crisis of 1982. The result was a much more pragmatic and less ideologically driven application of neoliberal policies in the years that followed. All of this, including the pragmatism, provided helpful evidence to support the subsequent turn to neoliberalism in both Britain (under Thatcher) and the US (under Reagan) in the 1980s.[21]

In New York, the lead was taken not by a dictatorship but by a series of exceptional apparatuses created by the city and state. Their legitimacy was derived from a fiscal crisis: the indebtedness of New York City. Beginning in late 1974 it had become clear that the servicing of debt alone was consuming about a fifth of the city's operating funds. Debt was sold on financial markets to investors at relatively low interest rates, on the assumption that the city was a credible borrower. Each year, however, the city was rolling over growing amounts of debt. This made it seem less likely that people would pay off their debts, with the result of reducing the attractiveness of public debt as marketable commodity.

The primary reason for this crisis was that in the post-war era, New York City's manufacturing base had been eviscerated, losing some 50 per cent of its labour force. The transition to a service economy could not sustain previous employment levels, nor did it make up for the growing shortfall in the city's finances. Indeed, the increasing numbers of unemployed people added to the welfare rolls, almost doubling the share of total city spending on welfare between 1961 and 1976. The growing number of public sector employees increased their bargaining power, and led to successful strikes by organised labour, thus acting as an upward pressure on costs. For much of the period before the crisis, these extra costs were borne by state and federal funding, but a significant component of it came from taxes on local businesses and property owners.[22]

The post-war agenda of liberal reform, particularly that initiated by Lyndon Johnson under the rubric of the 'Great Society', was

---

21. Harvey, *A Brief History of Neoliberalism*, pp. 8–9.
22. Lichten, *Class, Power and Austerity*, Chapter 4.

ideologically legitimised by the notion that America was an affluent society in which some of the profits of the boom should be shared with the poorest. In an era of recession, decline and accumulating deficits, that legitimacy waned. As the popular movements of the '60s retreated, American society moved to the Right. This presented an unusual opportunity to attack the consensus that underpinned the welfare state.

The existence of large public debts provided a hook on which an explanatory narrative could be fixed: too many services for the poor, too many bureaucrats to run them, union-driven labour cost increases, employers and tax base driven out of the city, and a corrupt and inefficient city management. All of this enforced by a progressive coalition in the city government, linking sections of the middle class and poor against the interests of the remaining productive population. To remedy the crisis, it was thus necessary to streamline the system, reduce the burden of the 'unproductive' population on the tax pool, and allow investors to keep more of their wealth to invest. Labour costs and taxation should be reduced to make the city more competitive, and attract more investors.

As indicated above, this narrative was not just a malicious fable. As long as the crisis was construed primarily as a fiscal one, there were elements of truth in the claim that welfare and wage bills were its primary cause. But looked at a different way, this was plainly inadequate. As mentioned, one major source of the crisis was the decline of the city's manufacturing base since 1950. This was hardly the fault of sponging 'welfare queens'. It reflected attempts by employers to suppress labour costs, conquer market share and rationalise production. As such it directs one's attention to the *generic elements of crisis* that are inherent in a normal capitalist economy, arising from intra-capitalist competition and the capital-labour relation, rather than simply exogenous pathologies that can be pinned on various unloveable scapegoats.[23]

---

23. On the concept of crisis, see Nicos Poulantzas, 'The Political Crisis and the Crisis of the State', in James Martin, ed., *The Poulantzas Reader: Marxism, Law, and the State*, Verso, London and New York, 2008.

And of course, while the austerians were right that the administration was irrational and inefficient, it would be difficult to imagine a modern capitalist state that is not. The modern state attempts to administer and process the irrationalities and antagonisms of a chaotic economy, but in doing so internalises them. Consider the following factors:

1) Periodic economic crises, which not only reduce tax receipts in the short term but result in pressure from business, on pain of investment strike, to reduce taxes on profits and investment.
2) The pressure from popular constituencies for services and provisions, based on expectations raised by the welfare state itself, which acts as a limiting factor on any fiscal cutbacks that state personnel are able to make.
3) The tendency for long-term regulative and growth strategies coordinated through the state to fail in the context of unplanned, competitive and antagonistic production relations.[24]

In such a context, any state is always only organising a temporary 'fix' that broadly helps to coordinate the various elements of a given economic space. The techniques of statecraft, whether Keynesian or neoliberal, can sustain a stable 'fix' for a reasonable length of time, but it is always suffused with irrationalities, and always potentially vulnerable to crisis or collapse.

The New York City case offers a lesson in the importance of ideology. The austerians took hold of elements of the crisis and gave it a recognisable, resonant interpretation that could quickly congeal as a 'common sense'. They didn't simply deceive or 'brainwash' people. (And I would invite the reader to visit a severe discourtesy on the next person who utters the word 'sheeple'.) They acted on elements of lived experience, and used their considerable resources to frame the discussion around that experience. Framing the issue as one of a fiscal crisis, they generated a significant amount of support for their goals.

---

24. On the crisis tendencies of the modern state, an excellent resource is Claus Offe, *Contradictions of the Welfare State*, Hutchinson & Co, London, 1984.

The unions and the left ran a counter-campaign, highlighting that the banks who were demanding austerity were making exorbitant money from the city. In doing so they highlighted one of the oddities of austerity politics – public advocates in tailored suits, telling studio anchors in some of the richest countries in the world that 'there isn't enough money to go round'. The obvious answer, from the perspective of unions and their allies, was to increase the tax base by raising levies on exorbitant financial wealth. But this gained little traction. The media were largely sympathetic to the agenda of union-busting and cutting services. The banks, for their part, carefully extruded themselves from the public debate, refusing to comment on the controversies with which they were intimately involved.

For the banks didn't merely shape the narrative; they partially *manufactured* the reality that the narrative described. The first stage of this was encouraging the city – through the Technical Debt Management Committee and the Board of Directors of the Citizen Budget Commission on which the banks were well represented – to get further and further into debt. The banks profited from this. The second was protecting their own profit margins when the debt became obviously unsustainable. They unloaded their own investments in the city's precarious debts, selling them off while the price was reasonably high. Simultaneously, they advised their small investor clients to purchase large amounts of this precarious debt. The third was insisting that in the event of the city's bankruptcy, the financial system should have first lien on the city's funds – which meant, of course, placing their needs above those of residents. The fourth was identifying the source of the problem as union militancy and social programmes, and devising a 'rescue' plan predicated on austerity. Fifth, the banks began to establish institutional mechanisms to convey their demands for austerity to the city's authorities, beginning with the Financial Community Liaison Group. Finally, and with aplomb, they gained effective control over the city's politics and finances through a series of institutions, above all the EFCB.[25]

The EFCB's dominant authority and planner was the investment banker, Felix Rohatyn, a known supporter of austerity. Inscribed in

---

25. Lichten, *Class, Power and Austerity*, Chapters 5 and 6.

its institutional make-up was a commitment to reforming the city's finances in order to service the debt. It had the power to nullify any agreement or union contract reached by the city. The bankers' effective *coup d'état* took power away from elected officials deemed too sensitive to popular constituencies, and above all too susceptible to pressure from public sector unions. As the job losses began, with over 8,000 teachers fired, the unions began to put up a defensive struggle. But their previous successes had been won as offensive battles in a growing economy. One result of success was the institutionalisation of bargaining mechanisms to avoid militant strike action. In this instance, they were fighting an intransigent state with new layers of authority amid a contracting economy and a fiscal crisis – and they were doing so with practices in place designed for negotiation rather than confrontation. The union leaderships largely accepted the need for some cutbacks and sought to protect conditions within that framework.[26]

This is not simply to participate in the familiar leftist pastime of decrying 'sell-outs'. Naturally, the union bureaucracies were highly conservative institutions. They were unlikely to develop a strategy that was capable of facing down the kind of entrenched power that the banks and corporations had – above all, their control of markets and operating capital. The unions' major potential strength was that the city depended on their labour, and a withdrawal could potentially be extremely disruptive for the companies that depended on its functioning. But by itself, this could be used to isolate and legally harass them. To win, they would have had to have activated much wider coalitions of poor and working people, alerting them to the dangers and above all posing an alternative 'rescue' plan. This the unions were not well-placed to do, and they were duly defeated.

Facing the Catastrophe

The New York City crisis was part of a wider conjuncture in which the US entered into a severe crisis affecting both its global dominance (Vietnam) and its economic competitiveness (Japan), in which the

---

26. Ibid.

post-war formula for growth and social peace was crumbling, and in which the old manufacturing industries were contracting. This was a moment of great danger for the US, and particularly its ruling class. It was therefore of tremendous importance that a number of parties began to take control of the elements in flux, recompose them, and in so doing begin the total, top-to-bottom transformation of the state, party politics, the economy and culture, producing a seemingly unassailable form of power.

Similar projects were subsequently rolled out across the US, Latin America, the UK, and Western Europe. If it was not clear at the time, it has certainly become clear since just how deep and wide-ranging these transformations are. We have been living through the consequences of a civilisational shift in global capitalism, a transformation that reaches into the foundations of the entire edifice. Some of the elements of this shift pre-date the dominance of neoliberalism, but neoliberalism gave a political name to the various projects that organised and gave shape to this new model capitalism.

One effect of the success of neoliberalism has been a long-term decline in the political and institutional participation of working class people. Membership of political parties, voting, and involvement in community organisation has shown a marked tendency to decline across the neoliberal core. What remains of the Left is often subculturalised, dependent on forms of sociality and on shibboleths that are exclusive and tend to repel new participants.[27] (The fragments of the old socialist Left in Britain sustains a facade of ostentatious 'normality' by consuming copious quantities of alcohol and evincing an interest in sport. But get them in a room together and watch them reveal their real alien selves, as they talk about 'the class', and hold forth on 'the dialectic'. I know. I am one of those people.)

Trade unions remain the largest democratic organisations in the neoliberal core, but their decline has not yet ceased. In 2013, after years of austerity, it was revealed that in the US the long-term decline of union density was accelerating:

---

27. For an acid account of this problem in the US context, see Bhaskar
Sunkara, 'Fellow Travellers', *Jacobin*, April 2013.

The percentage of workers in unions fell to 11.3 percent, down from 11.8 percent in 2011, the bureau found in its annual report on union membership. That brought unionization to its lowest level since 1916, when it was 11.2 percent, according to a study by two Rutgers economists, Leo Troy and Neil Sheflin.[28]

This is part of a global pattern. Union density fell first in the US, but followed in most industrialised countries and in all of Europe after 1978:

The United States was the first country to experience significant decline in union membership. In the 1950s US density was one-third of wage and salary earners in employment; in 1985 this proportion has been halved, and in 2000 it reached 13 per cent ... Other Anglo-Saxon countries have followed the US trend but at a slower rate. Union density in Canada dropped from 34.6 per cent in 1985 to 30 per cent in 2000.[29]

Nor is this just a secular decline resulting from the declining efficacy of unions and the incentives against organising built into an increasingly precarious labour market. It is linked to a process of 'bureaucratisation', as power has shifted from 'grassroots' members to a growing bureaucracy. A crucial example of this is the decline of the shop stewards movement in the United Kingdom, the defeat of its militant 'rank and file' by the Thatcher administration, and the emergence of a conservative form of leadership oriented by the doctrine of the 'new realism', according to which it was no longer realistic for the labour movement to do battle with the government of the day. Instead, members should look to their leadership to find 'influence' with an elected government to protect their interests. This

---

28. Steven Greenhouse, 'Union Membership Drops Despite Job Growth', *New York Times*, 23 January 2013.
29. Michael J. Morely, Patrick Gunnigle, David G. Collings, *Global Industrial Relations*, Routledge, Abingdon, 2006, p. 226; also Robert J. Flanagan, *Globalization and Labor Conditions: Working Conditions and Worker Rights in a Global Economy*, Oxford University Press, Oxford, 2006, p. 78.

placed most of the initiative firmly in the hands of the bureaucracy, which accumulated increasing privileges as a result.[30]

The effects of this are present in the response to the austerity projects in the most advanced, wealthiest economies. The relative passivity, in contrast to previous offensives, has been striking. A simple metric is the incidence of strike action in response to job losses, pay cuts and reduced conditions in both the private and public sector. Industrial action in the US has almost ground to a halt, despite some impressive actions such as the occupation at Republic Windows and Doors, or the anti-austerity battle in Madison, Wisconsin.[31] The figures for the period since 2007 compare poorly with the worst figures for any other decade since the Second World War.

In the UK, the major union mobilisations were impressively large, if a little late. The first major TUC action was a demonstration in 2011 in central London, involving hundreds of thousands of people. Coming some months after the student protests over tuition fees, it represented a broad cross-section of the organised working class, with large contingents of unorganised workers from all backgrounds. Paul Mason reported as follows:

> The massive fact of today was a very large demo of trade unionists and their supporters. I estimate upwards of 250,000. Probably less than half a million but certainly bigger than the Poll Tax demo of 1990, which I witnessed.
>
> The demographics were interesting. Unison – a union which has a reputation in the trade union movement for passivity – had mobilised very large numbers of council workers, health workers and others: many from Scotland and Wales; many from the north of England. Unite likewise, and the PCS seemed capable of mobilising very large numbers.
>
> What this means, to be absolutely clear, is people who have never been on a demo in their lives and in no way count themselves to be political.

---

30. Simon Hardy and Luke Cooper have described this process well. See their *Beyond Capitalism?: The Future of Radical Politics*, Zero Books, Winchester and Washington, 2012, pp. 65–82.
31. Taken from the Bureau of Labour Statistics (www.bls.gov).

I also saw many small self-selected groups not mobilised by unions: family groups, school groups, speech therapy groups.

My guess is that though this is the 'labour movement', a number of those marching would have voted Libdem also.

The sheer size and social depth of the demo is what all political strategists will now have to sit down and think about. I'm still thinking about it myself, but recording its size is important: the anti-war demo was bigger – maybe 1m plus – but this was certainly the biggest and most representative demo for 25 years.[32]

The next two major mobilisations were strikes, first by the smaller public sector unions on 30th June, and then with the largest unions involved on 30th November. They were formally motivated by cuts to public sector pensions, but the surrounding publicity made it clear that trade unionists considered this part of a more concerted attempt to obstruct the austerity agenda.

Both strikes involved the withdrawal of large amounts of labour: probably over a million people participated in the largest day of action. The disruptive impact was uneven. On 30th November, only 16 per cent of schools remained open, but the major airports functioned as normal.[33] Perhaps more important than the actual stoppage was the demonstration of the potential political power of such a large number of people. Nonetheless, it quickly became apparent that the trade union leadership were trying to negotiate a less onerous pensions deal, not spark a rebellion against the government's austerity agenda. They settled on a deal that, while not very good, was probably quite close to what they would have received from a Labour government.

This was quite an anti-climax considering the warnings of a 'winter of discontent'. But the reality is that this comparison was always absurd. The number of days lost to strike action in both 1978 and 1979 was 39 million. The total days lost to strikes in 2011, while higher than for some time, was only 1.4 million. And it was

---

32. Paul Mason, 'A Snapshot of the 26 March Demo', *BBC News online*, 26 March 2011, available at www.bbc.co.uk/blogs/newsnight/paulmason (all online sources cited in the notes were last accessed November 2013).

33. Helene Mulholland, 'David Cameron Admits Day of Actions was "Obviously a Big Strike"', *The Guardian*, 1 December 2011.

a temporary spike produced by two large one-day actions. The days lost to strikes the following year fell to an historically low level of just 250,000. Not only that but the strategic power held by groups of workers who went on strike in the 1970s – miners, steel workers, builders, transport workers – was considerably greater than that held by teachers, civil servants and nurses.

There was some feeling of 'betrayal' about the shoddy pensions deal, but the pressing question is why grassroots members accepted the union leadership's advice and voted for a bad deal. Surely this expresses precisely the factors mentioned above: accumulated political defeats for the unions, declining density, withering grassroots organisation and bureaucratisation, and political timidity.

Importantly, the overall disruption to the flow of profit from such action as does take place is negligible – so negligible that in most of the years since the credit crunch, the official statisticians don't even deign to put a precise figure on it: it's just less than 0.005 per cent. During these same years, the rate of profits for US nonfinancial corporations hit record highs, once the initial shock of the credit crunch was successfully fought off by state interventions. In November 2010, the *New York Times* reported:

> The nation's workers may be struggling, but American companies just had their best quarter ever.
>
> American businesses earned profits at an annual rate of $1.659 trillion in the third quarter, according to a Commerce Department report released Tuesday. That is the highest figure recorded since the government began keeping track over 60 years ago, at least in nominal or noninflation-adjusted terms...
>
> Corporate profits have been doing extremely well for a while. Since their cyclical low in the fourth quarter of 2008, profits have grown for seven consecutive quarters, at some of the fastest rates in history. As a share of gross domestic product, corporate profits also have been increasing, and they now represent 11.2 percent of total output. That is the highest share since the fourth quarter of 2006, when they accounted for 11.7 percent of output.[34]

---

34. Catherine Rampell, 'Corporate Profits Were the Highest on Record Last Quarter', *New York Times*, 23 November 2010.

The same pattern continued. *Forbes* magazine reported in December 2012:

> The numbers are in for Q3 and big business has $1.75 trillion worth of reasons to celebrate as these record-breaking results improved on last year's numbers by a stunning 18.6 percent—the largest after-tax profit quarter in the nation's history.
>
> And that's just for openers as total Q3 profits broke another record by accounting for a huge 11.1 percent of the U.S. economy.
>
> To understand just how big these numbers are, consider that the last period of economic expansion in America produced profits averaging 8 percent of the economy, significantly below their current percentage of GDP.[35]

This was actually typical of statistics coming out in the period, on both sides of the Atlantic. These profits were being achieved not so much through dramatic new growth, as through the drastic redistribution of what sluggish new income was produced. In the United Kingdom, between mid 2009 and 2010, 89 per cent of all new income went to profits. In 2011, economists at the Northeastern University in Boston found that 88 per cent of income growth in the US had gone to corporate profits and only 1 per cent had gone to wages.[36]

It might be argued, nonetheless, that this focus on trade unions misses something essential, which is the rise of protest politics.[37]

---

35. Rick Ungar, '3rd Quarter Corporate Profits Reach Record High – Worker Pay Hits Record Low: So How Exactly is Obama the "Anti-Business" President?', *Forbes*, 4 December 2012.

36. Steven Greenhouse, 'The Wageless, Profitable Recovery', *New York Times*, 30 January 2011; see also Andrew Sum, Ishwar Khatiwada, Joseph McLaughlin and Shiela Palma, 'The "Jobless and Wageless" Recovery from the Great Recession of 2007–2009: The Magnitude and Sources of Economic Growth Through 2011 and Their Impacts on Workers, Profits, and Stock Values', Center for Labor Market Studies, Northeastern University, Boston, MA, May 2011.

37. A statistically detailed – if, in my opinion, Pollyannaish – account of the rise of protests in the UK can be found in Adrian Cousins, 'The Crisis of the British Regime: Democracy, Protest and the Unions', *Counterfire*, 27 November 2011.

There is something to this. The emergence of new social movements from the mid 1960s reflected the politicisation of new corners of life, from households to higher education, sex to ecology. Initially, this raised the question of whether these movements were replacing traditional socialist class-based politics, or whether there was the potential for a powerful fusion of these absolutely heterogeneous elements with the labour movement. However, with the withering of the old Left, the decline of the unions, and the gradual disappearance of the tradition of community associations, a new question is posed: how is neoliberalism reconfiguring these social movements and limiting their possibilities?

Social movements tend not to leave much behind in the way of an institutional presence. Their gains are not converted into sustained organisation. And in the space vacated by the old forms of leftist and community organising there has sprung up a host of NGOs and think-tanks, which effectively act as political outsourcing firms for parties, governments, union leaders and sometimes even movements. Far from policies being democratically deliberated and decided upon, a technocratic layer of experts supplies the policy ideas, the ideological thematics, the dense intellectual justifications, and the ranks of eager, smart, well-turned-out PhD students ready to do something in the world besides teach other students.

At the extreme end of this tendency, NGOs actually instigate social movements in order to achieve what turn out to be quite moderate goals – some concessions on Third World debt, for instance. From Live 8 to the 'Big If', one finds the elements of a social movement convoked for a few weeks of celebrity-driven euphoria, culminating in a rock festival. Such events are notable for two features: 1) the focus on making politics a kind of entertainment, on the assumption that people will doze off *en route* unless they are constantly stimulated with music and funnies; 2) the emphasis on spectacle-positioning, that is, on working according to the conventions of the television news spectacle, creating an amenable 'feel good' product that necessarily disowns any disruptive intent.

I raise this because the vicarious, media-driven, euphoria-mongering aspect of contemporary politics is potentially a real barrier to success. Indeed, it concentrates and symbolises the tendency for some activists to leap from one campaign or issue to the next, blinded by the glare of events, without pausing to apprehend the slow-but-implacably-moving structural crisis that has been befalling us. I think that in the end this only leads to demoralisation and perpetual dysphoria, which can only be resisted by sober analysis.

The problem is that much of the traditional Left works, often with only the flimsiest disavowal, on the basis of a clutch of *historical guarantees*. The most important of these is that capitalism is always weak, decadent, hurtling toward its final crisis. The nastier it gets, the weaker it is. The major difficulties for the Left and the organised labour movement are purely subjective. Workers potentially have more power than ever before. These guarantees, though discreetly concealed, are the real effective force, rather like the 'little hunchback' in Walter Benjamin's fable about historical materialism. They enable one to tolerate any amount of necrotic cynicism about the state of the world without really coming to terms with it. One can recount with equanimity the painful realities of this crushing defeat, that human carnage, and then move on cheerfully – nay, *ecstatically* – to the next protest, provided one always has an underlying commitment that disavows the reality that these things signify.

Keeping the faith in a time of trouble for the Left hasn't necessarily meant being totally unworldly, but it has entailed a retreat behind dogma. It has meant being shut off from real developments – such as the total transformation of society since the 'glorious summer' of 1972 – that others became reconciled to by moving to the Right. But this little bundle of guarantees has ceased to function effectively. Capitalism's greatest crisis since the Great Depression *actually materialised*. And yet the result was not its breakdown, not its loss of political control, not the vaunted upsurge of the working class and the Left, but rather the strengthening of neoliberalism as offering the best solution to the crisis. Now there is no choice but to fully confront the catastrophe.

1

Class

Class is a communist concept. – *Margaret Thatcher*

Austerity is a class strategy.

But surely not? Aren't we simply obliged to make cutbacks now that times are tough? Who can honestly say that the country isn't broke? It would be nice to keep spending on all the gold-plated public sector pensions and bedroom scroungers and wasters, but there simply isn't enough money in the kitty, darlings. People will just have to pull their socks up. And tighten their belts. And figuratively rearrange other parts of parts of their apparel until the mess is sorted out.

And isn't 'class' itself something of a relic anyway, like the Madonna sex book, or a paid-for copy of London's *Evening Standard*? Or, at best, an abstraction remote from the messier realities of everyday life, like logging on to *Twitface*, sharing electrifying hoof fetish porn, and then ordering copious quantities of something via eBay to get richly and joyously shit-faced with? What sort of political fundamentalist bangs on about 'class' while the inhabitants of online heterotopias are obliviously fapping away together? What room is there for 'class' in these many proliferating life-worlds?

Despite these well-thought-out objections, and many more like them, I will insist on advocating the bland thesis that austerity is a class strategy. What else could it be? There is no socially neutral way of interpreting and resolving the multiple crises of production, politics and ideology triggered by the 'credit crunch'. There is no way that any strategy for confronting these problems could not respond to definite social interests, whether by proactively seeking to cater to them, reactively adapting to pressure, or anticipating and out-manoeuvring attempted obstructions. And these interests, whether concentrated in the form of the investment banks or the TUC, look a great deal like class interests.

The programme of austerity itself seems straightforward, as political scientist Mark Blyth explains: 'Austerity is a form of voluntary deflation in which the economy adjusts through the reduction of wages, prices, and public spending to restore competitiveness, which is (supposedly) best achieved by cutting the state's budget, debts, and deficits.'[1] Yet the case for this is not, on the face of it, a compelling one. The austerians maintain that a programme of cuts, properly implemented, can boost growth. The simple version of the argument is that government spending crowds out private sector spending. Freeing up wealth by cutting the tax burden should spur investment and dynamism. The more elaborate version is that cuts, or 'fiscal consolidation', will increase the confidence of investors, lenders and households. Knowing that the government's finances are being put in order, and that this is part of a sustained policy, they can look forward to a period of renewed growth, and thus expect more income in the future. As a result, households will borrow to spend, capital will invest, and banks will lend, thus precipitating a new phase of economic expansion. This is the austerity road to prosperity: expansionary austerity, as it is known.

The origins of this particular idea can be traced to an attempt by economists to theorise the practice of Western European governments undergoing fiscal consolidation in the 1980s. The argument essentially expressed the view of the West German government, or more specifically the Council of Economic Experts which advised it. It was the West German leadership in particular that advocated austerity as a basis for a future, leaner growth model for Europe.[2]

---

1. Mark Blyth, *Austerity: The History of a Dangerous Idea*, Oxford University Press, Oxford, 2013, p. 2.
2. Franceso Giavazzi and Marco Pagano, 'Can Severe Fiscal Contractions Be Expansionary? Tales of Two Small European Countries', *NBER Macroeconomics Annual* No. 5, 1990, pp. 75–111; U. Michael Bergman and Michael M. Hutchison, 'Expansionary Fiscal Contractions: Re-evaluating the Danish Case', *International Economic Journal* 24:1, 2009, pp. 71–93.

Of course, this contradicts the macroeconomic commonplace that cutting public spending at a time of economic weakness merely reduces consumer spending power and thus leads to lower growth. With lower growth, the state will take in less revenues with which to pay its debts. Any deficit will be increased, bond holders will become less confident of the state's ability to pay its debts and will thus drive up the cost of government borrowing, and the government will be forced into a new round of cuts merely to keep up its repayments. This sort of vicious cycle has already blighted Eurozone economies such as Greece and Ireland.

The empirical evidence from the UK, according to the Office for Budget Responsibility, seems to support the claim that austerity policies reduced growth in the UK in 2011–12 by around 1.4 per cent.[3] A 2011 IMF working paper points out that much of the empirical support for the claim that austerity is expansionary is based on studies which are biased by the inclusion of effects which don't arise from the cuts themselves but from external factors. The paper estimates that far from producing expansion, 'a 1 percent of GDP fiscal consolidation reduces real private consumption over the next two years by 0.75 percent, while real GDP declines by 0.62 percent'.[4]

Of course, the IMF has experience of implementing austerity, generally in the form of 'structural adjustment programmes'. These programmes have usually been applied to countries which urgently need to borrow. The result, almost invariably, has been to suppress growth. It is not even clear if the short-term goals of these programmes

---

3. Robert Chote, 'Letter from Robert Chote to the Prime Minister', Office for Budget Responsibility, 8 March 2013, available at budgetresponsibility. independent.gov.uk.

4. Jaime Guajardo, Daniel Leigh and Andrea Pescatori, 'Expansionary Austerity: New International Evidence', IMF Working Paper, July 2011. The Conservative-Liberal coalition government in the UK has embarked on cuts amounting to 4.5% of GDP by 2014–15. If the IMF's findings obtained here, then this would result in a 3.75% cut in private consumption, and 2.79% contraction in GDP in the years 2011–15. This figure does not include the impact of tax increases, or statutory price increases, such as the rise in VAT and the above-inflation increase in the costs of rail travel.

– improving the balance of payments and reducing inflation – are actually achieved. The research is ambivalent on this point. But the evidence is that, for as long as austerity is implemented, growth is reduced.[5]

However, it isn't good enough simply to point this out. The pro-austerity argument acknowledges the conventional 'Keynesian' macroeconomic wisdom, but nevertheless insists that in certain limited conditions fiscal austerity can be paradoxically growth-inducing: provided fiscal austerity is part of a *sustained reform*, provided private sector business really believes that the tax burden will decline over the long term, then it can be expansionary. It would be a mistake, both analytical and political, to dismiss this too lightly.

Further, it would be just as mistaken not to acknowledge that there is something eminently rational, from a certain point of view, about the desire to reduce the amount of public debt. Capitalist democracies have experienced a rising level of debt since the 1970s, linked to weak growth, higher structural unemployment, and a growing tax resistance on the part of the rich.[6] And since the banking crisis became a generalised economic crisis, this has turned into a sharp rise in public debt. US, UK and Eurozone states saw an increase in public indebtedness by between 20 and 40 per cent of GDP in the years from 2007 to 2009.[7]

There is a tendency on the Left to relativise about this, invoking by comparison the extraordinarily high levels of public debt during the

---

5. Adam Przeworski and James Raymond Vreeland, 'The Effect of IMF programs on Economic Growth', *Journal of Development Economics* 62, 2000, pp. 385–421; Joseph Stiglitz, a former 'free market' guru and social engineer of neoliberalism, makes the same point, although he attributes this to mishandling and indifference on the part of those imposing such policies. Joseph E. Stiglitz, *Globalization and Its Discontents*, W.W. Norton & Company, New York and London, 2002, p. 18.

6. N.B. Tax evasion seems like a too trivial description. What we have seen is a concerted class-wide effort on the part of the rich to resist taxation by national states as far as possible.

7. Robin Blackburn, 'Crisis 2.0', *New Left Review* 72, November–December 2011.

Second World War. But there are rational reasons why those same capitalist democracies sought to constrain public debt during the 1990s, and why they seek to do so now. The problem with austerity as a debt-reduction strategy is not *necessarily* that it identifies debt as an issue. It is, firstly, that it falsely and tendentiously blames debt on the tendency of democratic politicians and state bureaucrats to inflate budgets, rather than looking at the growing gap between the structural commitments of national states and the declining growth of national economies.[8] Secondly, to the extent that debt-reduction is a rational priority, it is not universally so. It is only rational if one accepts that capitalism, and specifically neoliberal capitalism, is the only game in town. And, if one accepts that the interests of elites – businesses and banks – are the most important interests in any national economy.

With this said, what kind of class strategy could austerity be?

No Such Thing as Society: Classes and Neoliberalism

A few words about the ontology of social classes are necessary before we proceed any further. This is because everything you know about class is just so much teak-hued horseshit. It isn't your fault. The attempt to obscure, or 'disappear', the concept of class is a deliberate, politicised mission.

Class, argued Mrs Thatcher, is a 'communist concept'. In a way, this is obviously preposterous. The valences of class are as varied as those of 'individual', 'nation', 'people' and so on. But as a disciple of Friedrich Hayek, Thatcher had a specific point in mind. This is linked to her more famous insistence that 'there is no such thing as society', only individuals and families.

What Thatcher meant is that at base, 'society' is composed of nothing but entrepreneurial, self-maximising units. Collectivities are at best 'thin' associations, or convenient fictions that enable people who are otherwise in permanent rivalry to work together for a shared

---

8. See Wolfgang Streeck, 'The Politics of Public Debt: Neoliberalism, Capitalist Development and the Restructuring of the State', *German Economic Review*, 2013, pp. 1–23.

goal. But these are potentially dangerous in that they can distort 'the market' and suppress individual freedom – which is nothing other than the freedom to be an entrepreneur. It is typical of neoliberal ideology that this rather bleak, brutal, Social Darwinist perspective of eternal struggle and competition is conveyed in the cuddly language of self-help books. Mrs Thatcher explained: 'I remember practically exploding when I heard some Americans talking about "the underclass," as if they weren't individuals with feelings. Each one is entitled to his own dignity, to develop his talents and abilities. Underclass? Socialist claptrap!'[9]

Intriguingly, US Congressman Rick Santorum attempted to emulate Mrs Thatcher in August 2013 when rallying the Republican faithful. He said:

> What does Barack [Obama] talk about all the time? The middle class. Since when in America do we have classes? Since when in America are people stuck in areas, or defined places called a class? That's Marxism talk. When Republicans get up and talk about middle class we're buying into their rhetoric of dividing America. Stop it.[10]

This was, again, tone deaf and absurd. The 'middle class' in US culture is the-class-of-no-class. It is a broad, indeterminate mass of people ranging from cleaners to stockbrokers, a pea soup in which classes are dissolved. Not only does this have nothing to do with the Marxist conception of class; it is not particularly relevant to *any* rigorous conception of class.

Why do the more doctrinaire neoliberals become so defensive about the concept of class that the mere use of the term is sufficient to get their sinewy lips beating together? The concept of class is dangerous for neoliberals because it cuts against the grain of their social theory,

---

9. Margaret Thatcher, 'Don't Undo My Work', *Newsweek*, 27 April 1992; Douglas Keay, 'Interview with Margaret Thatcher', *Woman's Own*, 23 September 1987. Both available at www.margaretthatcher.org.
10. Jillian Rayfield, 'Santorum: Term "middle class" is "Marxism talk"', *Salon*, 16 August 2013.

permitting that there are forms of collective organisation that have nothing to do with enterprise. It authorises the perpetuation and expansion of collective forms of organisation that lead to the gradual, ineluctable suppression of capitalist freedom. Which, to neoliberals, does look a great deal like communism. However, Mrs Thatcher's prohibition on even acknowledging class, denying it any ontological validity whatsoever, has been less successful than the claim that class is either a thing of the past, or not what it used to be. And there is an intelligible basis for this latter claim. Real developments in the neoliberal period rendered a certain way of talking about class, a certain language, dated. The figure of the 'shop steward' as the cutting edge of irrepressible subversion disappeared. The 'big battalions', those groups of workers whom no government could tame, were broken one by one. The seeming obviousness of certain connections – say, between workers and left-wing politics – was disrupted. The cultural salience of the male-breadwinner industrial workforce declined. Increasingly, classes were stratified by income, property, security and status, so that new social images of class could take root. These changes did not all simply result from neoliberal practices; rather, neoliberal politics took hold of existing tendencies and organised them. And the results have had profound consequences for how austerity is deployed, and resisted, today.

Aside from Thatcherite attempts to kill the notion of class, there are the more diffuse and routine representations of class within popular media and culture. This is the main centre of pedagogy about class (and race, gender, sexuality, and so on), and in so far as class is discussed, it is usually through morally informative anecdotes – the 'feral' underclass, the gluttonous badly eating poor, the lazy single mums on welfare, the 'chavs' and so on. I don't need to plough terrain already consummately tilled by Owen Jones.[11] Instead, what I want to do is advance a few general positions about class, and see how they can help us interpret the unfolding of the crisis and the ensuing austerity project.

---

11. Owen Jones, *Chavs: The Demonization of the Working Class*, Verso, London and New York, 2012.

1) Class is not an ethnicity, a tradition, or an interesting biographical trait. It has nothing to do with cloth caps and top hats. Or at least, that conception of class, linked to certain sentimental tea-towel memories of London's East End,[12] is not useful here. Neither is it merely a particular distribution of money or assets, or a job hierarchy. Those are merely outward attributes of class. The central question about class societies is who, through strategic control of the production process, nets the surplus produced in a society; and who, by being excluded from that strategic control, gets to produce all that surplus.

2) Class is nothing but a *relationship*. Another way to put this is to say that classes only exist in *relation* to one another. To take a couple of obvious historical examples: there could be no feudal nobility without a peasantry, as the former depended upon the latter to produce tribute, and the latter would not have existed as a subordinate class without the nobility; likewise, there could be no Roman slaves without citizens and nobles, and vice versa, since the toil of slaves provided the surplus from which a citizenry and a nobility could be sustained, while the slaves would not have existed as such without their rulers. This is important because there is a tendency for market researchers and sociologists to coin a profusion of new 'classes' without due rigour – the 'precariat', the 'new affluent', the 'salariat', 'the underclass', and so on. These 'classes' are described merely by a list of positive or negative attributes, without any sense given of their necessary relationship to other classes.

3) This relationship is necessarily, though not exclusively, *antagonistic*; otherwise it is hardly a class relationship. It is necessarily antagonistic, because the relationship revolves around the control of a surplus of wealth produced in society. In so far as a class rules, it disposes of this surplus in one way or another in its own interests;

---

12. You know how it is: back in the day, everyone knew the Queen Mum. We all ate jellied eels, everyone left their back door open without fear of burglary, and the Krays were rough sorts but only killed their own. This notion of the working class as a sort of dying ethnicity, a form of cultural nostalgia, is obviously suffused with dubious racial affect, cf. 'white working class'.

other classes have every reason to resent and resist this, unless the class which rules can somehow offer them an incentive to acquiesce. But it is not exclusively antagonistic, because for a society to work, for production to happen, for anything to be reproduced in its normal state, there has to be a minimum of cooperation.

4) Classes cannot exist without continually *reproducing* themselves. The process of this reproduction gives us a unique vantage point for understanding classes. Instead of trying to work out exactly who is rich and who is poor, as if class analysis was like a census, we can instead ask some more productive questions. What kind of society and what kind of relations are being reproduced, and by what mechanisms? How does this class help reproduce the society, and how does it reproduce itself in doing so? What role do states and other institutions play in this process of reproduction?[13]

In a capitalist society, the two major social classes are labour and capital. Capital, the ruling class, dominates by virtue of its strategic ownership of the means of production, its dominance of markets and the tremendous political and cultural strengths that come with these. It reproduces itself by investing its money in labour, equipment and infrastructure to produce commodities for sale, and generating a profit from the transaction. Labour, the working class, is dominated by virtue of its lack of any significant control of the means of production. It can only sell its labour power, its ability to work, in order to survive and reproduce itself. In this context, capital is able to ensure that a surplus – over and above what is required to cover wages, salaries and overheads – is produced and is able to recover this as profit.

That all seems simple enough. But beyond this it becomes quite complex. There is, after all, a significant multi-layered middle class, consisting of small business owners, professionals, lone traders, and junior and middle managers. These are layers of people who are separate from labour by virtue of their greater autonomy and authority, but who do not rule since they do not profit by extracting surplus from workers. Further, the main classes are divided among

---

13. Goran Therborn is convincing on this. See his *What Does the Ruling Class Do When It Rules?*, Verso, London and New York, 2008, pp. 133–8.

themselves. Capitalists compete, by definition; the system is driven by it. So the capitalist class divides over different sectoral interests, falling roughly into fractions representing – for example – manufacturing, commercial services and financial capital. Labour is increasingly stratified, from the least secure, lowest paid migrant worker to the reasonably well-organised skilled public sector worker. This is to say nothing of what happens when the intersections of gender, race, sexuality, nationality and so on are taken into account.

It follows from the above that the unity of classes – in pursuit of political objectives or whatever – can in no way be assumed. This is something that has to be continually worked on and produced. The Gramscian name for this practice is '*hegemony*'. This is not the same thing as domination. Rather, it involves a section of a class exerting political, intellectual and moral leadership within that class, or within an alliance of classes.

For example, during most of the twentieth century, the Labour Party in the UK 'spoke for' and 'led' the majority of the British working class, even though its organised core represented only a minority of that class. Deploying its philosophies (parliamentarism, social reform, national unity) and its apparatuses (the trade union leadership, the parliamentary party, the constituency parties), it organised utterly heterogeneous layers of the working class, alongside elements of the middle class, to achieve certain ends. This was never simple; such unity always had to be renegotiated, and reconstructed. Feminist, anti-colonial and anti-racist movements, for example, posed profound questions about the nature of this unity. And the shift to neoliberal statecraft, in which Labour has been unable to deliver any of its conventional palliatives to its working class base, has weakened its leadership claim.

There is a wider sense in which 'hegemony' is used, to signify a situation in which the dominant fraction of the ruling class achieves not only leadership of its own class, but also a degree of consent for its social goals within the wider society. It doesn't merely coerce and dominate but, by articulating an 'historic mission' which arouses broad support, secures actual leadership over other classes. For example, such a situation might be said to have obtained in the United States of the early Cold War, when the objective of defeating communism domestically and abroad won the support of a broad class alliance. This objective unified an otherwise fractious ruling class for a period of time, helped suppress and marginalise their domestic enemies, and won consent from workers who were promised free unionism and rising wages in contrast to the Soviet system of low wages and industrial tyranny.

Hegemonic projects therefore do not involve merely trying to defeat class enemies. They involve winning ideological and moral battles, shifting the popular 'common sense' and offering material incentives. Neoliberalism is such a hegemonic project, and austerity is part of its repertoire, its playbook for handling crisis situations.

This is worth stressing because of the tendency, noted in the introduction, to treat neoliberalism as if it amounted merely to 'free market fundamentalism'. And if one looks at the exoteric ideology of neoliberalism, it certainly appears as such. In the words of Colin Crouch:

> The principal tenet of neoliberalism is that optimal outcomes will be achieved if the demand and supply for goods and services are allowed to adjust to each other through the price mechanism, without interference by government or other forces – though subject to the pricing and marketing strategies of oligopolistic corporations.[14]

This looks like 'free market fundamentalism': let the market do its work, get the government out of the way. But in fact, a look at how neoliberal regimes have functioned, how neoliberalism has evolved in practice, suggests that it is far more comprehensive than simply an economic project. Neoliberalism is a multi-faceted effort to secure the unity of a class bloc behind the leadership of financial capital, to unite absolutely heterogeneous elements, and to shift the popular 'common sense'. The 'historic mission' of the neoliberal power bloc in the 1970s and '80s, its promise, was to resolve the deep crises of capitalism, to bring back law and order, and to allow people to go back to making money – by attacking the Keynesian and welfarist

---

14. Colin Crouch, *The Strange Non-Death of Neoliberalism*, Polity, Cambridge, 2011, Kindle edition, loc. 412.

instruments that they blamed for bringing about the malaise. To the extent that it succeeded, even its manifest injustices and failures were forgiven by many electors.

This is the sense in which I think it is useful to see austerity as a 'class strategy'. It is not simply a plot to grab wealth, but something far more sophisticated: it is an attempt to creatively respond to a crisis in a current configuration of power and class leadership by reorganising society and further shifting the popular common sense. This can best be understood by reviewing how we got to this impasse.

Neoliberalism as Crisis Management I

It is necessary to take a certain critical distance from the word 'crisis'. The term is indispensable, yet it is becoming a cliché and losing any connection with its heuristic value. There are three specific ways of talking about the credit crunch and the ensuing global breakdowns that illustrate this point:

1) *Technocratic.* The crisis is the result of a complex 'systems accident' in which multiple failures converge in unpredictable ways, akin to a natural disaster or a major industrial accident.[15] This is similar to the way in which the crisis of the 1970s tended to be explained as the result of a series of contingent factors such as the OPEC oil shock, often converging with peculiar national features such as militant unionism ('the British disease'). By implication, a crisis disrupts an otherwise harmonious equilibrium, which can be restored through various targeted 'fixes'. The indicated solution in this case is better markets with more adequate forms of regulation.

2) *Populist.* Put crudely, the crisis is the result of greedy bankers and/or the feckless poor, acting in self-centred and corrupt ways, with ruinous results for the ordinary, decent, hard-working majority of bozos. This is a morality tale with a moral solution: the bad people who caused this must be punished; the good people must be protected.

---

15. For a scathing critique of this conception, see Ewald Engelen et al., *After the Great Complacence: Financial Crisis and the Politics of Reform*, Centre for Research on Socio-Cultural Change, University of Manchester, Oxford University Press, Oxford and New York, 2011.

3) *Anticapitalist*. The crisis brings to fruition the generic elements of crisis which are always present in the capitalist system.[16] These tendencies arise from conflicts inherent in the system – the vertical conflict between capital and labour (class struggle), and the horizontal conflict between capitals (competition) – which result in chronic dysfunctions, whether in the form of underconsumption or a tendency for the rate of return on investment to fall. Each crisis of capitalism, if it is not resolved by a catastrophic destruction of capital through depression or war, thus allowing a new phase of dynamism to begin, tends to lead to stagnation and ongoing instability. The solution here is nothing short of an attack on capitalist class power, involving the redistribution of wealth, the socialisation of investment, and the democratisation of politics and industry.

These examples hardly exhaust the possible ways of talking about crisis. However, they hint at the complex web of connotations in which the term 'crisis' is embedded, and thus at the degree of unpacking that is required.

There is a risk of reductionism in each of these approaches. The technocratic answer, by treating the crisis as simply a disruption of an otherwise orderly and beneficial system, tends to avoid rigorous systemic analysis. While being able to prescribe specific policy remedies to restore some immediate functionality to the system, it also has an obvious apologetic function. The populist answer, taken up on both the Right and the Left in various ways, reduces social complexity to moral simplicity. It is perhaps unavoidable to talk about crisis in this way – blame, and resentment, are natural in a system of such rampant inequality. But it also seems to me that the Right benefits more from this mode of doing politics than does the Left. And I think there is, even in some of the most rigorous anticapitalist analyses, a tendency toward a form of reductionism that I would call *economic essentialism*, wherein the complex forms taken by capitalism are reducible to one or two central 'laws' or 'tendencies' of which these forms are merely expressions.

---

16. Nicos Poulantzas is excellent on the vital distinction between the mainstream approach to crisis as a temporary dysfunction and the leftist approach based on identifying the always present, generic elements of crisis in the system. See his 'The Political Crisis and the Crisis of the State', in *The Poulantzas Reader*.

The logic goes as follows. Capitalism is a system whose life-blood is profit: the only reason anyone produces anything in capitalism is because in the end it will result in a return higher than the original investment. When profit, the rate of return on investment, is depressed, then the system begins to enter into crises. Enterprises stop investing, staff are laid off, consumption declines and recession begins. And Marx identified a fatal tendency in capitalism for the profit rate to fall.[17] Although subject to various 'countervailing tendencies', this exerts a constant pressure toward crisis. And in a period when profits are generally low, the system is weak and unstable, and only resolves that weakness through mass destruction of capital (war or depression), or by methods which simply build new pathologies and instabilities into the system.

The vital next step in this argument is that, since the early 1970s, profit rates in the core capitalist economies have indeed been low by historical standards. The result is that growth has been sluggish, and the system has 'boomed' only through temporary expedients – financial innovations leading to stock market bubbles, the accumulation of massive amounts of debt, and so on. Yes, the system may have *looked* healthy at a superficial glance. But its health was built on precarity. And even if profit rates seemed to recover in the core economies after 1982 when the global economy began to recover, they were still significantly below the levels achieved in the 'golden era' of capitalism in the period from 1948 to 1973.[18] As a result, the tendency is to view the recession of 2008–9 as merely the culmination of a long period of crisis. As Kliman put it, 'the "booms"

---

17. For a useful short summary of this, see Marx's pamphlet 'Value, Price and Profit', available at http://www.marxists.org/archive/marx/works/1865/value-price-profit.

18. This argument is found, with certain variations, in Michael Roberts, *The Great Recession: Profit Cycles, Economic Crisis: A Marxist View*, lulu.com, 2009; Andrew Kliman, *The Failure of Capitalist Production: Underlying Causes of the Great Recession*, Pluto Press, London, 2011; and Chris Harman, *Zombie Capitalism: Global Crisis and the Relevance of Marx*, Bookmarks, London, 2009. Kliman's case is slightly different, in that his profitability figures don't detect any recovery in profitability for the US after 1982.

were just the flip side of the ongoing series of debt crises and burst bubbles, by-products of the same artificial "solution".[19]

The problems with this type of analysis are various. First, they treat the post-war 'golden era' as an historical norm for capitalism, when it was absolutely not a normal period. As David McNally puts it, these

> golden years of western capitalism … have become such a powerful cultural marker that even many left-wing critics treat them as the norm. If capitalism is not replicating the Great Boom, then they declare the system to be in crisis. Yet … the golden years were anything but normal; they represent a period of unprecedented dynamism whose return seems highly improbable.[20]

This misleading juxtaposition of post-1982 capitalism to pre-1973 capitalism can only result in an underestimation of the dynamism of neoliberal capitalism, and above all therefore *the reasons why it persists*. (If neoliberalism is an 'artificial' solution, then so is every solution which does not eradicate the crisis tendencies in capitalism.) By stretching the concept of crisis so that essentially it covers whole epochs, moreover, it loses what is specific to a crisis. Further, it tends to slide into the 'fundamentalist' reading according to which every crisis is worse than the last, and capitalism is always heading toward its final, consummating crisis.

This may have a lot do with his decision to exclude profits reaped by US corporations overseas, ignoring the role of US global dominance – or imperialism, as I still prefer to call it – in securing the material basis for American capitalist dynamism. If one excludes profits flowing in from, for example, South East Asia and above all China, then one significantly underestimates the health of the system.

19. Kliman, *The Failure of Capitalist Production*, p. 73.
20. David McNally, *Global Slump: The Economics and Politics of Crisis and Resistance*, PM Press, Oakland, CA, 2011, p. 27. In fairness, this does not apply to the explicit position of all of the economists cited above. Harman, for example, acknowledged the aberrant nature of the post-war boom. Nonetheless, it is hard to see how post-1982 capitalism can be judged as predominantly a period of crisis if not relative to the post-war era.

There is another problem. The late political economist Peter Gowan charged that mainstream economics had a tendency to treat the financial economy as somehow not part of the 'real' economy. The centrality of finance to the advanced capitalist economies, particularly the US, is hard to miss. In 1973, financial profits represented 16 per cent of total profits in the US economy; by 2007, the figure was 41 per cent.[21] Yet the value of financial assets often seems well out of proportion to any real value that they could have. By the mid 1990s the ratio of the value of financial assets to GDP in the US reached close to 950 per cent. It is also vastly out of proportion to any role the financial system might have as a support for the 'real' economy – as a sort of 'nervous system' for the economy, coordinating the allocation of capital and credit.[22] In 2001, the total daily turnover of international financial markets was $40 trillion, well above the $800 billion that would be needed to support transactions and investment flows in the 'real' economy.[23]

In this light, it is easy to see why finance is seen as less 'real' than other sectors of the economy. The only source of real value in the economy is work. It is people labouring to produce commodities.

21. Ibid., p. 86.

22. This metaphor is used by David Harvey to sum up the potential power that resides in the credit system in terms of ironing out the imbalances and 'contradictions' in the economy, ensuring a quantitative match between production and consumption. For example, credit can be allocated to enable house-building, while also simultaneously allocated to ensure that house-buying is financed. In this sense, the financial system could achieve the seemingly impossible task of securing the *general* interests of capitalism against the specific interests of individual businessmen. It never actually achieves this, of course, precisely because even if it were possible to calculate the general interest of capital, the financial system has a tendency to generate a new layer or fraction of bankers and financiers with their own distinctive interests. See David Harvey, *The Limits to Capital*, Verso, London and New York, 2007, pp. 284–6.

23. See Peter Gowan, 'Crisis in the Heartland', *New Left Review* 55, January–February 2009; figures from Doug Henwood, *After the New Economy: The Binge … and the Hangover That Won't Go Away*, The New Press, New York, 2005, p. 191; and Harvey, *A Brief History of Neoliberalism*, p. 161.

Financial 'innovators' are, from this perspective, 'unproductive'; they don't make anything, but merely invent ways to extract value produced elsewhere in the form of rent. In this view, the creation of imaginary values – for example, blowing stock market bubbles – is a purely secondary and parasitic activity in a capitalist economy. From this one could conclude that the financial system is a dangerously under-regulated casino which menaces productive capital with its speculative activity (a populist view shared by some on the Left), and that the unleashing of this system is a reckless attempt to inject dynamism into a sluggish system.

There is some truth in this view of a dangerously liberated financial system, but it misses a number of important points. From the point of view of investors, profit is just a stream of additional money gained by putting an initial sum of money into circulation as capital. It doesn't matter greatly to them whether they get their profit by making light bulbs or selling credit default swaps. And it doesn't matter if the value they extract ultimately comes from labour performed in a business set up in Michigan or in Shenzhen.

And while finance is often counterposed to the 'productive base' of an economy, the growth of finance has made that productive base more efficient in many ways. By incorporating ever more workers and businesses into the system, through investments and debt, it exerts a powerful disciplinary force.[24] As more workers become tied to debt, they have an incentive to accept higher workloads and longer working hours, to produce more for less. As businesses become

---

24. As Albo, Gindin and Panitch put it: 'The populist distinction between the financial and "productive" sectors relies on a one-sided notion that finance speculates in pieces of paper, and not in providing real goods and services ... The financial system is necessary to capitalism's functioning, and innovations in financial markets provide competitive advantages for the originating capitals and the states they reside in. The discipline finance has imposed in the neoliberal era on particular capitalists and workers has forced, moreover, an increase in U.S. productivity rates by way of increased exploitation, the more intense use of each unit of capital, and the reallocation of capital to sectors that are more promising.' Albo, Gindin and Panitch, *In and Out of Crisis*, p. 33.

leveraged, they have an incentive to restructure and become more productive, or else be forced out of business. The growing efficiency of manufacturing industries, achieved through rationalisation and downsizing, led to the concentration and centralisation of capital, accompanied by a shift in employment patterns as most workers ended up working for smaller businesses which were themselves up to their eyeballs in debt and thus very responsive to the imperative to extract the maximum profit from their labour force. One effect of all this is to have stratified the workforce increasingly between a core stratum of 'skilled' workers, a peripheral workforce of 'unskilled' clerical and menial workers, and a large layer of increasingly precarious workers.[25]

Furthermore, the incorporation of the mass of the population into the financial system, incubated in the post-war era but taking off with the advent of neoliberalism, both legitimised the system and supported expanding mass consumption even when real wages did not increase. It gave workers a vested interest in the health of the system, as their ability to consume depended significantly on the well-being of finance. The financial system had to be 'democratised' in a thin sense for this to happen, by degrees incorporating not just the affluent middle classes but eventually even the poorest workers. By 2000, households' outstanding debt as a proportion of personal disposable income reached 97 per cent: an all-time high, and higher than the 80 per cent reached during the second half of the 1980s. Household savings also declined drastically in the US during the 1980s and the 1990s. From 1950 to 1980, household savings were at a ratio of 8–9 per cent. In the 1990s, they averaged 5.2 per cent, and in the years 2000–3, 1.9 per cent. People had spent more and more of their available income. Barring this development, it is estimated that household consumption would have grown 1 per cent slower in the years 1992–2000.

---

25. A useful discussion of these trends in the workforce can be found in Andre Gorz, *Critique of Economic Reason*, Verso, London and New York, 1989, pp. 64–7; I wrote a brief article about this: see Richard Seymour, 'Hovis's Zero-hours Strike and the Wrong Way to Share Out Work', *The Guardian*, 22 August 2013.

Linked to all this is America's global domination, which some intrepid pundits began, after September 2001, to venture was an empire. The extension and Americanisation of the global financial system, and the internal articulation within Wall Street of the many local financial markets to which it is connected, ensures that a constant flow of value and profit is directed toward investors in the United States. The growth of the world economy during the neoliberal period was, by historical standards, relatively robust. Much of this growth was concentrated, however, in newly industrialising economies – above all, China. The construction of what Peter Gowan called 'the Dollar-Wall Street regime' helped ensure that much of the value generated in these growing economies, with their *vast* supplies of cheap labour, was accumulated by US investors.[26]

All of this is to stress that it simply isn't adequate to trace the origins of the crisis down to certain 'fundamentals', particularly as the crisis itself was not immediately induced by a traditional pattern of over-accumulation. The role of the financial system itself, so central to neoliberal capitalism, must be examined. As Albo, Gindin and Panitch put it:

> The onset of the crisis in 2007 was not rooted in any sharp profit decline or collapse of investment. In 2006–07, profits were at peak and an investment expansion appeared to be forming – productivity continuing to increase substantially in manufacturing, labor compensation lagging, and low-cost inputs being imported from export processing zones in Mexico and China. Rather it was rooted in the dynamics of finance.[27]

Those left-wing accounts which refuse to treat the financial system as a primary factor in the credit crunch and global recession, instead

---

26. See Leo Panitch and Martijn Konings, eds., *American Empire and the Political Economy of Global Finance*, Palgrave Macmillan, Basingstoke and New York, 2008; on the dynamism of the global economy in the neoliberal period, and the benefits yielded by capital in the core economies, see McNally, *Global Slump*, pp. 37–60.

27. Albo, Gindin and Panitch, *In and Out of Crisis*, p. 42.

attempting to reduce everything to more 'fundamental' sources of crisis within the system, may have a certain validity. They are attempting to deepen their critique, to speak about the role of capitalism as such in generating the crisis. They are also side-stepping the vulgar populist interpretation of the crisis as one caused by the borrowing of the feckless poor. But they are in their way as reductive as those which treat the crisis as a technical accident. I want to indicate a slightly different way of interpreting the crisis, which respects the specific effectivity of many causes, and which recognises that while there are generic elements of crisis built into the system, these are also part of the health of the system, and the emergence of a crisis cannot ultimately be reduced to them.

Neoliberalism as Crisis Management II

At the most general level, the world economy was prone to a sharp, devastating economic breakdown because the neoliberal growth pattern was most advanced in the dominant global economy, that of the United States. There, all of the most unstable and antagonistic aspects of neoliberal practice were concentrated within a single national economy.

The dominance of central bankers and finance capital did not emerge, fully formed, in the 1970s under the impress of neoliberalism. It had been gradually incubated within the post-war order. Even while finance was relatively subordinate to other sectors of capital, the material infrastructure that would enable it to thrive was being constructed by New Dealers and empire-builders.[28] Moreover, certain long-term developments were essential to enable the dominance of finance capital in the neoliberal era, including: the development of a modern financial system coupled with the emergence of modern corporate capitalism at the turn of the twentieth century; the growing division between management and ownership in the major firms; the emergence of interlocking directorates in which large

---

28. On this subject, the master-work is unquestionably Leo Panitch and Sam Gindin, *The Making of Global Capitalism*, Verso, London and New York, 2013.

firms are connected through shared directorships and thus able to attain a 'business-wide' purview.[29] The institutional configurations made possible by these changes allowed major financial apparatuses to become the nerve centres of capitalism, exercising decisive strategic control over the allocation of investment capital and the goals of production.

However, it was a crisis of the post-war system, beginning with the breakdown of the gold standard in 1971 and the shift to fiat currency as the global currency, that enabled a decisive shift in the locus of capitalist class domination. In the post-war era, New Deal state intellectuals had helped develop the global financial architecture known as Bretton Woods. At the centre of this, naturally enough, was a system of fixed exchange rates for currencies anchored to the American dollar, which was itself pegged to the value of gold. This made sense for as long as national economies wanted US products, and needed dollars to purchase them with. However, the dynamism of rival capitalist economies – which post-war US policies had been designed to promote – combined with declining US competitiveness, led to its first trade deficit in 1971. It produced a sharp decline in the value of the dollar, as countries that had previously sought dollars to purchase US products suddenly needed less of the currency. President Nixon responded to the looming crash by taking the dollar off the gold standard. At first, this was tentative, and took place against significant resistance within the state. However, by 1973 it was clear that Bretton Woods was at an end.[30]

The wider macroeconomic elements of the 1970s included a crisis of profitability, soaring unemployment, high inflation, and

---

29. Useful on these developments are Gerard Dumenil and Dominique Levy, *The Crisis of Neoliberalism*, Harvard University Press, Cambridge, MA and London, 2011; John Scott, *Corporations, Class and Capitalism*, Hutchinson & Co, London, 1979, Chapter 4; Michael Useem, *The Inner Circle: Large Corporations and the Rise of Business Political Activity in the US and UK*, Oxford University Press, Oxford, 1986; Michael Schwartz, ed., *The Structure of Power in America: the Corporate Elite as a Ruling Class*, Holmes & Meier Publishers, Inc., New York, 1987.

30. McNally, *Global Slump*, pp. 88–92; Panitch and Gindin, *The Making of Global Capitalism*, pp. 122–31.

the emergence of public debt as a salient issue. The traditional remedies of implementing wage and price controls, of subsidising or nationalising failing industries, no longer availed in resolving these problems. The post-war alliance between large Fordist producers and sectors of labour, co-organised by the state, had been predicated on wages rising alongside productivity. But in the context of declining profitability, firms sought to suppress labour costs. This induced waves of labour militancy and a breakdown of the authority of management which the old corporatist remedies were not able to contain.

This is where financial institutions, the upper strata of the capitalist class and the emerging New Right were able to coalesce around a decisive shift in the configuration of power. The class objectives of finance capital – militant counter-inflation as the basis for macroeconomic stability; sound money; liberalisation of capital controls and re-regulation of markets in the interests of investors; the tightening of market discipline; reduced welfare expenditures – provided the coordinating points for a new class alliance. It is wholly wrong to describe neoliberalism as merely the ideological expression of these class objectives, as some do, but one might say that there was an elective affinity between the dominance of finance and the implementation of neoliberal governmentality.[31]

One result of this shift was the further mass integration of workers into the financial system. This happened in a number of ways. Workers who had been used to receiving wages in cash were increasingly remunerated through their bank accounts. The suppression of wages, necessary for the revival of profitability after 1982, was achieved with the aid of union-busting, lean production and some strategic offshoring of production.[32] As a result, the mass consumption previously sustained by wages had to be sustained through debt instead. Housing became an asset against which to borrow – the deliberate rationing of housing kept prices soaring, and allowed people to take out second and third mortgages. This mass

---

31. This is a crucial mistake made in Dumenil and Levy's *The Crisis of Neoliberalism*, p. 18.

32. Kim Moody, 'Contextualising Organised Labour in Expansion and Crisis: The Case of the US', *Historical Materialism* 20:1, 2012, pp. 3–30.

debt-driven form of economic expansion was most advanced in the US from 1997 to 2007, above all in the new housing sector. By 2000, over 40 per cent of new-home mortgages were financed with down payments of less than 10 per cent of the value of the home, while it was estimated that a quarter of new mortgages were being issued to people who were broke.

The re-regulation of financial activity enabled the profusion of new financial devices. In particular, derivatives played a crucial role:[33] the notional value of the derivatives market increased from $1.2 trillion in 1992 to $4.2 trillion in 2007.[34] The result of the collapse of Bretton Woods had been that, for the first time, the global currency was completely unmoored to any real commodity. The value of international currencies became volatile, and currency trading became a hugely lucrative market, increasing in value from $15 billion in 1973 to $3.2 trillion in 2007. This explosion in the global money supply, and the volatility produced by the new situations, fuelled a similar explosion in new financial instruments based on managing the risk.[35] The key derivatives in the 2000s were those based on the value of *debt*. These included:

1) The credit default swap market – in which more secure institutions such as hedge funds are paid to guarantee a creditor against losses in the event that the debtor defaults.
2) Collateralised debt obligations – a form of mortgage securitisation.

The product being sold in these cases is a kind of 'flutter', a bet on whether a debt will be paid. With techniques of labyrinthine complexity, the financial industry sliced, diced and tranched debts,

---

33. Briefly, a derivative is a financial contract whose value derives from that of an underlying asset or price. For example, a trader might purchase the right to buy an asset, such as gold, at a certain value at a future date. This is speculation, a bet, on the future value of gold. If the value of gold suddenly soars, the trader can buy the asset at the agreed value and make a windfall.
34. McNally, *Global Slump*, pp. 19 and 94.
35. Ibid., pp. 93–7; David Harvey, *The Condition of Postmodernity: An Inquiry into the Conditions of Cultural Change*, Blackwell, Oxford, 1989, pp. 141–72.

distributing risks and rewards across portfolios. The higher the risk in any debt portfolio, the higher the chances of significant gains or losses given any credit event.[36] The real value and risk of these assets became impossible to calculate. When Lehman Brothers collapsed, they told Treasury officials in no uncertain terms: 'We have no idea of our derivatives exposure and neither do you.'[37]

Significantly, this process had to be facilitated by national states (see Chapter 2 for more on this). States had to break the power of opposing forces, such as trade union militants; they had to restructure capitalism and flush out 'unproductive' capital; they had to reorganise the role of the banks, and overhaul the tax and welfare system. This entailed a shift in the relationship between state power and class power, above all the mutual interpenetration of state power and financial power.

Banks and financial institutions had long played a strategically central role in the interlocking directorates that dominated the highest level of production in the US. The key institution regulating the financial sector in the US has, since 1913, been the Federal Reserve. The legislation creating it was drafted by bankers, and the emerging institutional matrix cemented state and corporate power together. Of course, the Bretton Woods agreement institutionalised the American

---

36. Susan George explained how this can work with a useful example. Suppose you have a grand to invest as you see fit. Bernie Madoff offers you an opportunity to invest in a scheme that will give you a return of 10% on top of your original investment over a year. You would make an extra £100. But if you wanted to really speculate, you could borrow a further £9,000 from the bank and invest ten grand on the deal. That way, your return would be – minus 5% interest on the loan – about £550, or 55% of your original investment. But if the investment goes badly, you might make less. And if the market fails, or Bernie escapes to the Bahamas, you lose everything, and still owe the bank £9,000 plus interest. Credit, the mere act of borrowing, raises the stakes in the transaction. And the more you borrow, the higher the potential profit, and loss. See Susan George, *Whose Crisis, Whose Future?*, Polity, Cambridge, 2010, pp. 35–6.
37. McNally, *Global Slump*, pp. 19 and 94; Tony Norfield, 'Derivatives and Capitalist Markets: The Speculative Heart of Capital', *Historical Materialism* 20:1, 2012, pp. 103–32.

state's role in organising the foundations of the US financial system and its internationalisation. The value of the emerging institutions of the IMF and World Bank to US capitalism was something that even the Nixon administration, having junked Bretton Woods, was compelled to recognise. A Treasury memorandum in 1973 highlighted their role in 'achieving US political, security and economic objectives with particular respect to the developing nations'.[38]

In the context of the crises of the 1970s, as indicated in the introduction, the mutual interpenetration of the state and financial institutions was accelerated in the interests of crisis management. The institutionalisation within the state of the objectives of finance was signalled above all by the 'Volcker shock',[39] which was intended to demonstrate that the state was serious about implementing austerity and sticking to it. Indeed, the very prominence of the Federal Reserve among the state apparatuses, when previously it had been a relatively anonymous institution, was itself a sign of the growing dominance of finance. By 2007, it was in the United States that the vessels of financial capital most visibly protruded into the apparatuses of the state, just as Wall Street began to tank.

Finally, this new arrangement had to achieve some form of ideological and cultural legitimacy. It was one thing for neoliberals to take on and destroy significant bastions of organised class opposition – Reagan's defeat of the PATCO workers, Thatcher's defeat of the miners – and quite another for them to achieve a certain *popular consent* to their goals. This is not the same thing as popularity (see Chapter 3), but there had to be a complex of ideas which made it more acceptable to at least a decisive minority within the population.

---

38. Quoted in Panitch and Gindin, *The Making of Global Capitalism*, p. 154.
39. Wherein, starting in 1979, the chair of the Federal Reserve, Paul Volcker, drove up interest rates on lending to a staggering 21%. This not only squeezed investment and consumption: it broke the back of organised labour, and also ensured that overseas debtors were suddenly in dire straits and in need of IMF assistance to manage their debts. This enabled the neoliberal restructuring of indebted countries, above all in Africa and Latin America. See Naomi Klein, *The Shock Doctrine: The Rise of Disaster Capitalism*, Penguin, London, 2008.

A cross-class coalition of sorts had to be assembled. Mrs Thatcher assembled the support of sections of business, the lower middle class and a chunk of skilled workers, including a large number of trade unionists. Reagan achieved a similar sort of coalition, the working class 'Reagan Democrat' being a critical element of his support.

It was in the United States that the ideology of neoliberalism enjoyed its greatest successes in academia, which in turn provided the personnel for banks, the Federal Reserve, regulators and the White House. And it was in the United States that finance capital, Wall Street, enjoyed its greatest cultural run. In the dominant ideology shared by politicians, regulators, bankers and academics, the growth of the financial system was – remarkable as it may seem now – seen as a stabilising factor, as well as a democratising force.[40] But this was far too esoteric, and frankly far too stupid, for mass audiences. For them, it was more important that the mundane business of buying and selling acquired an aura of libidinised, testosterone-fuelled, gladiatorial struggle, with spectators wolfing down coke on the terraces.[41]

Culturally, perhaps, Wall Street was at its peak during the 'Bubba bubble' – that mad, hedonistic, irresponsible decade known as the 1990s, in that mad, hedonistic, irresponsible, incontinent continent known as North America. Everyone was supposed to be getting rich off the 'New Economy', with venture capitalists popping up all over the place. Wall Street was certainly flooded with cash, and IPOs (in which investors plough money into an upstart entity in exchange for a share of future profits) were bankrolling a wave of flimsy new ventures that would mostly go under by the turn of the millennium. However, most workers who gambled on investments lost, and approximately 80 per cent of the increase in financial net worth was accounted for by the top 20 per cent of the population.[42] The main

---

40. On elite views of financialisation as a democratic process, and a source of moderation in the economic cycle, see Chapter 2 of Engelen et al., *After the Great Complacence: Financial Crisis and the Politics of Reform*.

41. About which, let's be honest – if this was actually how Wall Street worked I wouldn't be writing this book.

42. Henwood, *After the New Economy*.

way in which people actually related to financial institutions was through crushing relations of debt and dependency.

The first sign of the emerging crisis was the popping of a bubble in US housing in 2005–6, but the trends leading most directly to crisis were visible from the late 1990s. It was in 1997 that corporate profitability in the nonfinancial sector started to decline again after a long recovery since 1982.[43] It was also in the late 1990s that households began to press against the limits of their ability to raise income by working more. (Working hours per employee in the US are the highest among the core capitalist economies.) And from that period real wages began to fall.

Debt-financing became the basis for continued growth in roughly the decade after 1997. This was encouraged by the Federal Reserve's response to the 2001 recession, which was to maintain extremely low interest rates, enabling Americans to keep spending by refinancing their mortgages or cashing in on the equity value of their property. It also meant that financiers could blow a speculative bubble in mortgage-related securities and collateralised debt obligations. But as the Federal Reserve started to raise interest rates, in the interests of keeping a lid on inflation, payments on mortgages – particularly subprime mortgages – rocketed. This resulted in a rise in non-payment, a decline in new entry into the housing market, and a collapse in the issuance of new mortgage-backed securities. Since the housing bubble had worked in part through the splicing of mortgage debt with other types of securities, the malaise quickly spread through financial networks to other sectors, internationally. By 2007, the banking system was grinding to a halt and threatening to halt production with it.[44]

This conveys something of the configuration of power and production that crunched to a temporary halt in 2007. This configuration was what David Harvey would call a 'spatio-temporal

43. This decline was reversed following the recession of the early 2000s. See Andrew W. Hodge, Robert J. Corea, Benjamin J. Hobbs, and Bonnie A. Retus, 'Returns for Domestic Nonfinancial Business', Bureau of Economic Analysis, June 2013, available at www.bea.gov.

44. Albo, Gindin and Panitch, *In and Out of Crisis*, pp. 61–3.

fix'[45]: a way of organising different aspects of production to help manage, for some period of time, the crisis tendencies in capitalism. It was one implemented under the class leadership of financial capital, and obtained a remarkable degree of consent among political parties, academics and experts, business coalitions, and even sectors of the wider population. It defeated most of the opposition. It generated a significant return to profitability for businesses over a long period of time, accompanied by relative macroeconomic stability on some indices (inflation and GDP growth above all). It sustained expanding consumption for the majority even while the distribution of wealth was increasingly unequal. These are some of the reasons why the consensus among elites prior to 2007 was so complacent.

Yet, if this 'fix' was one way of managing the crisis tendencies in capitalism for a period of time, it was also one which introduced new crisis tendencies, new forms of precarity, particularly in the form of a tempestuous financial sector. This, and the dependence of the whole system on finance, is why the 'golden rule' of the neoliberal era has been that the banks must be protected at all costs. And this elite consensus, while shaken up by the credit crunch, was ultimately not displaced by any alternative purview. There were no rival class forces sufficiently well-organised to challenge the dominance of financial capital and to impose an alternative solution. Thus, neoliberalism persists, and is deepened, in the form of 'austerity'.

Example 2: Austerity in the US – Wisconsin and the Workers

One of the major effects of neoliberalism was the defeat, through a series of set-piece battles, of old forms of class politics rooted in industrial struggles. The only serious bastions of union recognition and collective bargaining were in the public sector, with the result that in the US in 2012 some 37 per cent of public sector workers were unionised compared to just 6.9 per cent in the private sector.[46] Public sector workers do not occupy strategically central positions

---

45. David Harvey, *The New Imperialism*, Oxford University Press, Oxford, 2003.

46. 'News Release', Bureau of Labor Statistics, US Department of Labor, 23 January 2013, available at www.bls.gov.

in industry, and therefore their strikes don't always have the same impact as those, for example, in the car industry. But one advantage they do have is that their work has to do, one way or another, with the political administration and control of large populations. When they strike, it is political in a way that it is not obviously the case when private sector workers do so – it directly implicates the government in a social struggle. And if their strike gains public support, it can become the basis for something more like a militant social movement.

This is how it was in Wisconsin.[47] Governor Scott Walker had been elected on a Republican ticket, on the basis of a promise to deal with the state's deficit. This became the basis for the state's own austerity project. Whereas austerity is driven largely by the central government in the UK, in the US it has been initiated at the level of local states and cities, *particularly* where aggressive GOP politicians have been elected with a significant slice of business support. Governor Walker was one of a string of new Republican administrators elected in the November 2010 general election, benefiting from the demoralisation of Obama's voters, who largely declined to turn out and re-elect Democrats. Walker's major business backing came from the 'FIRE' sector (finance, insurance and real estate), construction companies, healthcare, and the notorious billionaire 'Tea Party' sponsors, the Koch Brothers.[48]

---

47. Some useful articles inform this section. See particularly Paul Street, 'May Day Special: The Wisconsin Rebellion and its Limits in a Global Context', *New Left Project*, 1 May 2011; Andrew Cole and Phil Gasper, 'Wisconsin: From the Uprising to Recall Walker', *International Socialist Review* 83, May 2012; Dan LaBotz, 'A New American Workers' Movement Has Begun', *The Bullet*, Socialist Project, E-Bulletin No. 466, 21 February 2011. Also, see Paul Buhle and Mari Jo Buhle, eds., *It Started in Wisconsin: Dispatches from the Front Lines of the New Labor Protest*, Verso, London and New York, 2012; and Michael D. Yates, ed., *Wisconsin Uprising: Labor Fights Back*, Monthly Review Press, New York, 2012; and a useful pamphlet: George Martin Fell Brown, 'The Battle of Wisconsin: History and Lessons from the Working-class Revolt of 2011', *Socialist Alternative*, February 2012.

48. Andy Kroll, 'Wisconsin Gov. Scott Walker: Funded by the Koch Bros.', *Mother Jones*, 18 February 2011; see, for a detailed breakdown of his funding in 2010, *Follow The Money*'s profile of Walker available at www.followthemoney.org.

Walker waited only until February to announce the programme – spending cuts, tax cuts for business and, more importantly, rolling back the collective bargaining rights of public service employees. As ever, this was far from being simply a 'cuts' package: it was part of a comprehensive, ideologically informed[49] attempt to shift the balance of class forces in a direction favourable to business.

One of Walker's earliest measures, for example, was to privatise the Department of Commerce, replacing it with the Wisconsin Economic Development Corporation. The important thing about this move was that it transferred responsibility for the economic development of the state outside of any direct democratic accountability to the state senate, to a panel of businessmen and the governor. Of course, the workforce implementing these decisions would be non-union, but this was a small win compared to the huge bounty of handing a government department over to private capital. The neoliberal hostility to democracy had always been articulated in public in the form of an apparent naive belief in the competitive efficiency of 'markets' and the private sector. This is exactly how Walker sold the move, as an attempt to increase the commercial vitality of the state. In fact, Governor Walker's austerity programme led to a slump in the growth of new employment,[50] and the Corporation ended up, *quelle surprise*, being mired in corruption and the mishandling of public funds.[51]

This is not to say that reducing the deficit was not a goal for Walker. His implementation of corporate tax cuts was taken by left-wing opponents as evidence that the deficit was merely an excuse to wage an 'ideological' attack on unions. Of course, Walker's neoliberal apologists would argue that cutting business taxes removes the burden of the 'unproductive' layers of society on the 'productive' members, gives capital room to invest and thus, by generating growth, increases

---

49. N.B. 'ideologically-informed' does not mean 'stupid', 'non-pragmatic', etc. See Chapter 3.

50. Jack Norman, 'Job Slump is Walker's fault', *Milwaukee-Wisconsin Journal Sentinel*, 1 April 2013.

51. See 'Wisconsin Economic Development Corporation', Legislative Audit Bureau, Report 13, 7 May 2013, hosted on www.sourcewatch.org.

the state's tax receipts. Likewise, the attack on union bargaining rights may be treated as simply 'ideological'. But in fact, the attack on bargaining rights did cut costs, simply by destroying the bargaining power of public sector workers and forcing them to accept much worse conditions.[52] The point is that what Walker wanted was not just any solution to the deficit; he wanted one commensurate with the social goals of his major backers in industry and financial services.

Walker's aggressive opening move did not go unchallenged. It provoked a ferocious response, beginning with a University of Wisconsin-Madison rally on 14th February, three days after Walker's announcement. The next day, tens of thousands of protesters entered the Capitol building in Madison. On 17th February, 14 senate Democrats fled the state in order to prevent a quorum necessary to vote on Walker's Bill. The protests in the ensuing days were consistently in the tens of thousands, and swelled to 70,000 on 19th February. The largest protest took place on Saturday 26th February, with 100,000 turning out. On 1st March, Walker gave his budget address at a livestock feed manufacturers, almost two weeks after scheduled, while the Capitol building was occupied and thousands filled the main plaza outside.[53]

The movement that developed was militant and rowdy, but did not resemble the devoutly wished for 'rank-and-file' union movement which characterised previous waves of working class militancy. As Dan La Botz wrote, this was 'not your grandfather's working class', not the good old days of industrial workers who built the Industrial

---

52. See, for example, 'Kaukauna Area School District Projects $1.5 Million Surplus After Contract Changes to Health Care, Retirement Savings', *Appleton Post-Crescent*, 29 June 2011; Larry Sandler, 'Milwaukee to See Net Gain From State Budget', *Milwaukee-Wisconsin Journal Sentinel*, 8 August 2011; Elizabeth Hartfield, 'Wisconsin Recall: Fact-Checking the Walker Economy', *ABC News*, 5 June 2012.

53. See full speech at 'WPT Full Coverage – Gov. Scott Walker's 2011 Budget Address', 2 March 2011, available at youtube.com. An excellent account and contextualisation of the protests that day can be found in Lee Sustar, 'Who Were the Leaders of the Wisconsin Uprising?', in Yates, ed., *Wisconsin Uprising*.

Workers of the World, forged the American union movement, and won their rights in the depths of the Depression:

> The new labour movement that is arising does not start in the industrial working-class (though it will get there soon enough), it does not focus on shop floor issues (though they will no doubt be taken up shortly), it is not primarily motivated by a desire for union democracy (though it will have to fight for union democracy to push forward the leaders it needs). And it does not, as so many American labour movements of the past did, remain confined to the economic class struggle (though that too will accelerate). It is from the beginning an inherently labour political movement. The new movement that is arising does not focus on the usual issues of collective bargaining – working conditions, wages, and benefits – but focuses rather on the political and programmatic issues usually taken up by political parties: the very right of workers to bargaining collectively, the state budget priorities, and the tax system which funds the budget.[54]

Until this point, the 'Tea Party' movement had begun to dominate the narrative about the recession and the future development of American capitalism. As in previous waves of neoliberal austerity, the offensive was fronted not by the rich themselves, but by a cross-class coalition cemented by a broadly neoliberal ideology drawing directly from Hayek among other sources. The movement, though instigated and supported by wealthy backers – the Koch Brothers again being prominent among them, alongside the tobacco industry[55] – was not simply an 'astroturfing' operation. It had a real social basis – albeit one overwhelmingly composed of older, wealthier and white citizens – and is best understood as a conservative *social movement* largely predicated on a middle-class response to the recession. Racism and the fear of 'socialism' were – as they so often have been in American

---

54. LaBotz, 'A New American Workers' Movement Has Begun'.
55. Amanda Fallin, Rachel Grana and Stanton A. Glantz, '"To Quarterback Behind the Scenes, Third-party Efforts": The Tobacco Industry and the Tea Party', *Tobacco Control*, January 2013.

politics – intermingled to toxic effect. To the Tea Partiers, the credit crunch and ensuing recession were the result of incompetent borrowing by the poor, particularly African Americans; and now 'they' had got one of their own elected to take even more dough away from hard-working Americans. In effect, the Tea Party rallying cry was 'black people caused the crash and are going to take all our stuff!'[56]

What Wisconsin signalled was the first counterpoint to this reaction, and the beginning of the cycle of social movements and protests against austerity that would culminate with Occupy. Ideologically diffuse, the Wisconsin protests were united around some core goals, above all the protection of public services and union bargaining rights. At its peak, it seriously disrupted the workings of the local state, overcame police repression, mobilised tens of thousands, enjoyed widespread support and gained worldwide attention. It totally changed the dominant narrative about the recession, so that for the first time the actions of the rich and their representatives were being questioned.

Unfortunately, the Wisconsin movement was a germinal, inchoate uprising, up against some very seasoned and determined opponents. This is where the question of hegemony comes up again. There were attempts to organise the militants and the Left in the labour movement, such as the 'Kill the Whole Bill Coalition', intent on opposing the entire sweep of austerity and not just specific measures. There was also an intervention by the radical National Nurses United, which provided a left-wing interpretation of the struggle and the necessary strategy. But the 'Kill the Bill Coalition' was too narrow, and the radical nurses unions had no significant base in Wisconsin. They could mobilise a few thousand people, but they were unable to match the forces of the big unions.[57]

In so far as the movement had a political organisation or structure it was provided by the union bureaucracy and the Democratic

---

56. Zachary Courser, 'The Tea "Party" as a Conservative Social Movement', *Society* 49:1, January 2012, pp. 43–53; Kate Zernicke and Megan Thee-Brenan, 'Poll Finds Tea Party Backers Wealthier and More Educated', *New York Times*, 14 April 2010.

57. See Sustar, 'Who Were the Leaders of the Wisconsin Uprising?', in Yates, ed., *Wisconsin Uprising*.

Party. The unions were conservative and narrowly based, and the Democrats were in the end another party of business. The unions stopped mobilisations after 26th February, and told police they no longer supported the occupation of the Capitol building. Since the Wisconsin Professional Police Association had come out against Walker's Bill, the change of tactics on the part of the unions signalled to the cops that it would be permissible to start clearing out protesters.[58] They rejected a principled anti-austerity strategy, insisting that it was necessary to build a broad coalition and that this would involve concessions on public spending. It seems probable that, like the Democrats, the broad coalition they wanted to form was with those more cautious Republican senators who hadn't signed up to Walker's high risk war on labour.[59]

Either way, this actually demonstrated not the breadth but the *narrowness* of their social base.[60] Had the unions been more firmly implanted in the working population, with a greater density of representation, it would have been harder for them to pull back from defending expenditures on public services. Had they been interested in assembling the broadest coalition, they would have championed the political demands of the non-union members allied with them rather than simply attempting to reach a compromise that protected their own bargaining rights. As it was, sticking to the issue of bargaining rights allowed Walker to pit unorganised private sector workers against the supposedly 'entitled', 'privileged' public sector workforce.

In contrast, the ruling class, or leading sections of it, were able to efficiently organise a response to the mass movement in Wisconsin.

---

58. Ibid.

59. On the 'moderate' Republicans, and the strategy of Democrats and union leaders, see Patrick Marley, Jason Stein and Daniel Bice, 'At Wisconsin Capitol, Week Ends in Gridlock, Frustration', *Milwaukee-Wisconsin Journal*, 25 February 2011; and Sarah Seltzer, 'In Letter, Wisconsin Democrats Demand Compromise, Offer to Meet Walker at Border', *Alternet*, 7 March 2011.

60. On the narrowness – indeed unpopularity – of unions in the US, see Doug Henwood, 'Walker's Victory, Un-sugar-coated', *LBO News from Doug Henwood*, 6 June 2012.

And they were determined: the Koch Brothers responded to weeks of protest by insisting they were defending 'freedom' and warning 'we will not step back at all'.[61] They had not only the Republican Party, but also a variety of PACs, lobbies and think-tanks – such as the American Legislative Exchange Council,[62] or Americans for Prosperity – through which slushed cash from the largest US corporations. They had sympathetic news networks amplifying their already ample voices. And they had at least some activists, 'Tea Party' supporters and others, willing to 'counter-protest' for Walker, as well as a passive base of supporters who were willing to come out and vote for the Republicans again if necessary. Finally, they understood that their major strength was the weakness of the unions, which was itself partially the product of previous successes for neoliberalism. The crisis gave them a unique opportunity to expose that weakness and to accentuate it.

In the end, Walker cleared the Capitol building of protesters and passed the Bill without quorum. The movement dissipated, and the Republicans were emboldened. The fleeing Senators returned, and the Democrats and unions began a strategy of channelling the movement into a parliamentary and legal process. A prolonged judicial challenge to the repeal of unions' collective bargaining rights was launched, alongside a campaign to recall Wisconsin senators and ultimately Governor Walker. The unions made the turn to recall elections early on, calling for protesters to go home and start planning for these rather than protesting in the capital. The AFL-CIO, the main union confederation, organised a large 'We Are Wisconsin' coalition focused on winning recall elections, with 12,000 activists involved.[63] Both strategies ultimately failed. A federal court of appeals backed up the collective bargaining law. But more importantly, the Democrats

---

61. Shawn Doherty, 'Koch Executives Vow to "Continue to Fight" in Wisconsin', *The Capital Times*, 25 February 2011.
62. *The Nation* magazine has run a series of articles exposing ALEC's political activities on behalf of business, beginning with John Nichols, 'ALEC Exposed: Rigging Elections', *The Nation*, 12 July 2011.
63. Matthew Rothschild, 'Accountability in Defeat in Wis.', *The Progressive*, 7 June 2012; Fell Brown, 'The Battle of Wisconsin'.

failed to retake the senate and Governor Walker was re-elected with a bigger margin.

Why did the recall strategy fail? Some have referred to rigging, and there was probably an element of gerrymandering, inasmuch as redistricting ensured that in the 2011 recalls the party that won less than half the vote (the Republicans) gained more than half the seats contested (five of eight).[64] However, that doesn't explain the debacle in 2012.

I would venture, as a beginning, two key factors. First, the dissipation of the movement and the turn to a parliamentarist strategy gave the Republicans space to breath. A protracted campaign of civil disobedience, strike action and community campaigning might have achieved what Democratic lobbying could not, and split the Right. It might have hardened up the position of the unions in bargaining, and weakened the resolve of the axe-wielders. But the recall campaign was pitched specifically as an alternative to any creative protest strategies. Thus, with the movement gone, the Bill already pushed through, and a Republican majority in the senate, there was no reason not to proceed with gusto. The unions had proved their weakness. Second, the Democrats, having watered down their message, were in the same bind as in November 2010 when Walker won in the first place; in order to govern effectively as a party of the pro-capitalist centre, they needed their working class base, but they couldn't offer them very much. By the time Walker went into the recall election, he had a war chest full of money and could boast to supporters that he had reduced the deficit and busted the unions as planned, thus shoring up his support. He was thus able to add more voters than the Democrats could. It didn't help that the Democratic candidate was the same weak candidate who had already lost to Walker, but he was saddled with a losing campaign anyway.

In all, the timidity, legalism and top-down strategy of the union leaders and their Democratic allies were no match for the sheer venal ruthlessness and corruption of their Republican and business opponents. As Doug Henwood put it:

---

64. See Brendan Fischer, 'Wisconsin's "Shameful" Gerrymander of 2012', *PRWatch*, 4 February 2013.

It's the same damn story over and over. The state AFL-CIO chooses litigation and electoral politics over popular action, which dissolves everything into mush. Meanwhile, the right is vicious, crafty, and uncompromising. Guess who wins that sort of confrontation? ... Suppose instead that the unions had supported a popular campaign – media, door knocking, phone calling – to agitate, educate, and organize on the importance of the labor movement to the maintenance of living standards? If they'd made an argument, broadly and repeatedly, that Walker's agenda was an attack on the wages and benefits of the majority of the population? That it was designed to remove organized opposition to the power of right-wing money in politics? That would have been more fruitful than this major defeat.[65]

The Wisconsin moment passed, but some of its constituent elements could be found again, enlarged, in the Occupy movement. It was in this movement, which encompassed occupations and protests in 70 major US cities and 600 local communities, that the thematics of a new type of movement and a new type of militancy emerged. Their 'broad coalition' was 'the 99%' rather than 'the 1%'. Their tactic was also an attempt at prefiguration: direct democracy, in a form that accommodated the most heterogeneous elements while attempting to safeguard against oppression or exclusion. Their answer to backroom deals and legalistic politics was riotous defiance. Occupy was defeated too, but as I will argue in the concluding chapter, it showed us some of the means by which, eventually, we will *not* be defeated.

---

65. Henwood, 'Walker's Victory, Un-sugar-coated'.

2

State

State-monopolized physical violence permanently underlies the techniques of power and mechanisms of consent: it is inscribed in the web of disciplinary and ideological devices; and even when not directly exercised, it shapes the materiality of the social body upon which domination is brought to bear. – *Nicos Poulantzas*.[1]

Picture the scene. Whitehall, November 2010. You're one of those pupils who will be sitting your GCSEs[2] this academic year. Your hair has writing in it, literally shaved into it. Your cap has writing on it. Your T-shirt has writing on it. Your arm has writing on it – perhaps one of those 'tattoos' you make with a sewing needle and a pen.[3] You're here to protest against the trebling of tuition fees and the abolition of the Education Maintenance Allowance which allows working class kids to go for higher education – because it's an act of war on your future and that of your younger siblings. And the first thing that strikes you, amid the tensely euphoric crowds, trails of coloured smoke, and mounted policemen, is a carbon steel, lever-lock, expandable baton. The sort of weapon that is explicitly advertised for sale as virtually indestructible. It will crush your skull before it suffers a single scratch.

The impact is hard, the most painful blow that you have ever experienced, and it splits your cheek open. You collapse, lie down

---

1. Nicos Poulantzas, *State, Power, Socialism*, Verso, London and New York, 2000, p. 81.
2. For American readers, that's like when you have your SATs before 'graduating'.
3. Just fill in the blanks yourself, please, because I obviously have no idea what young people are like these days.

and clutch your face in agony, fortunate not to be trampled by the fucking horses. You can feel blood congealing and sticking your fingers together. Before there's the chance of medical attention, there's been another mounted police charge, and a battalion of fresh police vans has hovered slowly into view, blocking off all exits. It's a kettle. You have to settle in for a few hours of dubstep and crap alcohol, at sub-zero temperatures. Eventually your bleeding ceases and your head stops thumping, but by the time you are allowed out of the kettle, in a slow, painful, single file, you feel weak and nauseous. You are starving. You need to piss. You are shivering. You haven't seen anyone you know for hours. The dubstep has been replaced by something else. 'You say you want a revolution?' The wrong John Lennon. Who the *fuck* is playing that? As you get waved through an elaborate exit formed of heavily armed riot police, with a photographer openly taking close up snaps, a voice of indeterminate origin says '*now fuck off, oik – we're trying to get rid of the nanny state*'.

This is essentially the image of the neoliberal state today. Its self-representation is that it is downsizing, constantly – eviscerating itself, slashing its own wrists. Nor is this an emergency disposition: supposedly the neoliberal state has been trying to get out of people's way since it was a cheeky glint in Hayek's eye, seemingly knowing when it isn't wanted. And yet the second there is any serious contest, any major conflict of interests, it is the state that appears, settling matters with sudden, maniacal, swingeing violence. Ninja-like, it conceals itself in the sinks, recesses, dark corners and perimeters, emerging for swift bouts of exemplary force, only to retreat from view just as quickly.

Obviously, this is not how it actually is. The neoliberal state is everywhere, from the Jobcentre Plus to the PFI firm, from the primary school league table enforcers to the council lawnmowers. It is present in the contracts between employers and workers, between sellers and buyers, between landlords and tenants. It is there when people are born, and still there when they are buried. It is overseas and underground, in the air and in the gutters. While the state may not be 'seen', there is never a moment when it actually disappears.

In the introduction, I cast doubt on the notion that austerity is chiefly about reducing the size of the state, or reducing the total spending on sustaining it. This is not to say that the austerians aren't interested in keeping a lid on or cutting expenditures. In certain cases, such as Greece and Ireland, this has been a marked priority. But it is to say that they are at least as interested in reconstructing the state and its role in social organisation as in reducing its size. In the interests of spelling this out further, I here advance five initial theses about austerity and the state:

1) The state is not withdrawing from 'the economy' – it is never absent from 'the economy'[4] – but changing its mode of presence in it.

2) The state's cost-cutting commitments are subordinate to its crisis-management commitments. The latter tends to make the former difficult, because in a crisis economy the costs of investment are relatively higher and businesses are more reluctant to invest what capital they do have. Therefore, it falls on the state to find ways to incentivise production, and get capital moving.

3) State institutions act within a context of ongoing social conflicts and struggles. These social struggles – whether over class, race, gender, or sexuality – exert pressures on the state. The policymaking of different state institutions must therefore respect the relative strengths of the opposing sides. They may, because of their history and institutional make-up, favour one side or other, but they must also register the balance of forces as they exist. This determines the form that crisis management takes. It cannot simply be a tight, well-organised conspiracy that takes no account of popular demands and interests. As I will suggest in Chapter 3, this makes the acquisition of consent, of ideological legitimacy, very important.

---

4. Mariana Mazzucato has demonstrated the centrality of what she calls the 'entrepreneurial state', not just in providing the 'conditions' of production with infrastructural expenditures, and not just in providing research and development funding and various incentives for firms, but in making the critical early investments that businesses are too timid to make, opening up new areas of capital accumulation, developing new industries and making markets work. See *The Entrepreneurial State: Debunking Public vs. Private Myths in Risk and Innovation*, Anthem Press, London and New York, 2013.

4) The form of crisis management adopted must be understood in terms of the dominance of banks and corporations within the state. There is no socially neutral way of resolving a serious crisis. To imagine that there is a neutral index of economic management such as GDP growth or full employment, is mistaken. Even the ordering of these priorities reflects different interests – notably, what immediately distinguished the neoliberal state from the post-war Keynesian state was the former's prioritising of counter-inflationary goals against the latter's prioritising of full employment. In the last instance, what matters to capital is the rate of profit on investment, whereas what matters to labour is the wage rate and the amount of work done to get it. These are incommensurable interests. Thus, when the state embarks on an austerity agenda, it is plainly not sufficient to deride it as unpragmatic. What is not pragmatic from the point of view of ensuring full employment may be perfectly pragmatic from the point of view of consolidating the social power and financial interests of the dominant banks and businesses.

5) The relationship between a state and the society that it regulates is permanently characterised by dysfunction and disequilibrium. This is not to take the absolutist position that nothing short of the complete overthrow of the system can resolve a given crisis. Different forms of crisis management have been effective in more or less provisionally resolving past crises. But each resolution is itself unstable and brings its own problems. Post-war welfare and nationalisation policies, by raising expectations of the state, and by empowering subaltern groups, in the long run actually deepened the potential for crisis. Neoliberal 'market discipline', as the solution to that crisis, contained an in-built propensity toward chronic instability, particularly as it empowered the financial sector's 'creativity'. Therefore, the success and viability of austerity should not be judged in terms of whether it abolishes all of the imbalances and dysfunctions in an economy. It should be judged relative to the social goals of the class or group that favours it, and the degree to which it provisionally, temporarily, helps meet those goals. These might include forestalling rival projects from opposing classes, consolidating political control,

installing a reasonably sustainable economic 'fix', and so on. The generic elements of crisis and disequilibrium will continue to be present, but the sources of power will be preserved. Austerity is thus a *hegemonic project* that is worked out within the state.

To these theses I will add one observation: capitalist states are, over the long term, tending to become more authoritarian. This trend has always been obscured by a straightforward 'Othering' strategy: during the Cold War, the virtues of the 'liberal' 'tolerant' and 'permissive' 'West' could be extolled just as political freedoms were being curtailed, because the alternative was supposedly the gulag; during the 'war on terror', the same virtues were sung to the heavens just as states were eroding civil liberties. In this chapter, I address the subject of authoritarianism in relation to the fiscal crisis. But it is important to distinguish this *general drift* from purely conjunctural crisis regimes of the sort that both Greece and Italy have experienced, or indeed from a crisis of the state as such. Neoliberal regimes have reduced their democratic capacities by outsourcing previously accountable functions to businesses, quangos and unelected bodies. They have increased the scope of state authority. But, while obviously related to the general re-organisation of states under neoliberalism, the interludes of technocratic dictatorship in Greece and Italy, and the police mobilisations against social movements there and elsewhere, are distinct processes. There is *no necessary sense* in which an economic crisis results in a crisis of the state and the attempt to resolve it in an authoritarian manner. The example of Greece, dealt with in this chapter, makes this distinction clear.

In what follows, I will describe the political crises to which austerity politics is offered as a response, and link this to the processes of neoliberal state formation.

The 'Fiscal Crisis' of Modern States and the 'Crisis of Authority'

Two specific inter-related political crises are linked to the austerity project: a 'fiscal crisis', and a 'crisis of governability'. If the appearance of a 'fiscal crisis' of the state is supposed to legitimise a process of austerity, the cause of the 'fiscal crisis' is said to be the moral turpitude and social irresponsibility of those who will suffer from austerity. Their refusal to be governed, to withdraw their demands on the state, provokes a 'crisis of governability'.

Is there, though, a sense in which permanent 'austerity' is an in-built feature of modern welfare states? Is there a permanent 'fiscal crisis'? Certainly, the current period of retrenchment builds on practices already well-established by national states. Welfare state cutbacks have been a constant theme since the Thatcher-Reagan era. In France, Jacques Chirac and Alain Juppé led an austerity front in the early 1990s, though they were effectively seen off by a militant labour response. In the United States, Bill Clinton ended 'welfare as we know it' with a series of reforms cutting benefits and forcing recipients to work for their miserly allowance. In Canada, the Chretien government embarked on a drastic cuts programme, whose success in erasing the country's deficit is often cited as a case of 'expansionary austerity'. In Germany, Gerhard Schroeder implemented 'Agenda 2010', an austerity package aimed at improving the competitiveness of German capitalism, beginning in 2003 – the cost of this was a split in Schroeder's Social Democratic Party.

The primary justification for *these* austerity projects was summed up in the term 'globalisation': meaning that the world economy was more integrated, more competitive, and national states less able to offer traditional welfare protections without losing an edge against rivals. Governments argued that if they taxed businesses and incomes too much, they risked sapping funds for investment and growth; further, they might drive businesses abroad and thus only deplete the basis for welfare even further. The only way to fund welfare and public services was to stimulate sufficient economic growth so that the ker-ching ker-ching of daily commerce would send tax revenues pouring into government coffers.

This gets at *some* important parts of the truth, but the problem is that 'globalisation' is not one single, coherent trend but rather a complex of ambiguous developments, and there is little evidence that these processes in themselves prevent redistributive taxation and spending strategies. However, there are a number of endogenous factors that appear to have applied severe constraints to welfare spending: the declining productivity and growth of the advanced capitalist economies; the shift to service economies; and the demographic shift to an older population.[5]

This appears to suggest that, as long as these trends continue, *fiscal crisis* is endemic to modern states. Indeed, the sociologist James O'Connor suggested something like this in 1973,[6] just as the post-war social compromise was falling to pieces and before the fiscal crisis of New York city. According to O'Connor, there was a long-term 'tendency for government expenditure to outrace revenues', and this was rooted in two basic functions carried by the state: accumulation and legitimation. The first included practices designed to ensure effective demand in the economy, contain recessions, make production more efficient, stimulate research and development, shut down or devalue failing capital, modify the institutional basis of the economy, and generally ensure the *social reproduction* of capitalism. The second involved the organisation of consent, the mediation of class struggles, the creation and maintenance of the shared cultural and social space within which production takes place, and the deployment of material incentives to encourage consent. For O'Connor, the costs of these functions tended to rise beyond the ability of the state to recover revenues. This was ultimately rooted in a conflict between democracy and capitalism because, no matter how many economic functions the state takes on, the control of profits remains in private hands, and the state cannot take control of these profits in the interests of carrying out its legitimation functions without seriously curtailing capitalist power.

This is plausible, but the problem with this type of analysis lies in the attempt to infer state behaviour from various 'functions' that it supposedly has to perform for the social system to be viable. First of all, the evidence is that a lot of what states do is dysfunctional to the system as a whole. It is, for example, at the very least debatable

---

5. A useful discussion of these trends can be found in Paul Pierson, 'Irresistible forces, Immovable Objects: Post-industrial Welfare States Confront Permanent Austerity', *Journal of European Public Policy* 5:4, 1998, pp. 539–60.

6. James O'Connor, *The Fiscal Crisis of the State*, Transaction Publishers, New Brunswick NJ, 1973.

whether the US invasion of Iraq was functional to the world capitalist system, or even to US capitalism. Second, there are precisely no economic functions that can only be fulfilled by the state: historically they have all been carried out by the state, the private sector, or both in certain variations. This includes infrastructural development, social reproduction, monetary management and so on.

We therefore need to ask: why do states take on any economic functions at all? Part of the explanation might be that certain necessary economic sectors are insufficiently profitable for private industry to carry them out. But this only provides part of the explanation. After all, nationalised health services would potentially be extremely profitable if turned over to private insurance, pharmaceutical and surgical equipment companies. It is arguable that socialised health performs a *legitimation* function, and this is true, but even here a privatised health system can be part of a relatively stable, legitimate capitalist democracy. It could also be argued that certain functions are so important that, where they are taken on by one fraction or sector of capital, the pursuit of short-term profitability is too destructive and dangerous to the social fabric that it threatens the system as a whole.[7] This presents a more promising answer, but only if qualified in an important way.

If, as I have argued before, the state is nothing but a strategic field of force in which is condensed the class and political relations present in the wider society, then any 'line' within the state must emerge from the 'play' of opposing forces. So when the state organises class hegemony, it necessarily does so by organising a 'variable field of compromises between the dominant and dominated classes' (Poulantzas). As such, the only way in which the state can attempt to claim to represent a *general interest* (whether of capitalism or 'the nation') is through the dominance of a *particular interest* – that of a hegemonic fraction of capital, which dominates a 'power bloc' consisting of allied classes and fractions, which itself is full of antagonisms. This means that any decision as to what economic functions to take on, and when, ultimately comes down to a messy

---

7. This, with qualifications, is the analysis given by Poulantzas in *State, Power, Socialism*, pp. 180–2.

compromise between rival forces the ultimate result of which is weighted toward the hegemonic fraction of capital.

Taking this *continually negotiated, constantly constructed* aspect of state intervention into account, we can pose the question of where the limits to public spending arise from. O'Connor is ultimately correct that a downward pressure is imposed by the need to keep the control of profits in private hands. However, as one of O'Connor's early critics pointed out,[8] the limit at any given historical moment must be determined, at least in part, by the productivity and profitability of the economy itself. A decline in growth and profits would lead to a concomitant decline in revenues, all else being equal. The willingness of business to support 'high' expenditures would also decline.

The dilemma is all the deeper in that it is precisely the loss of growth and profitability that leads to a need for *more* state intervention so that the scale of state expenditures soars relative to a stagnant or contracting economy. Whether it is covering the costs of unemployment, sustaining economic demand, subsidising or taking over failing businesses (banks in the current situation), suppressing wage claims or controlling inflation, a dysfunctional economy tends to require deeper state intervention. The history of public spending in the UK during the twentieth century seems to bear this out. Outside of the spikes arising from war, the high points in public spending, when it was generally somewhat above 40 per cent of GDP and often closer to 50 per cent, coincide with periods of serious economic crisis.[9] In such circumstances, states can certainly borrow against future growth to manage an acute crisis, but this is sustainable *only if they have a viable growth strategy*. And that growth strategy must factor in not just dominant ideologies and bureaucratic-technical analyses, but also a series of sustainable social compromises.[10]

---

8. Fred Block, 'The Fiscal Crisis of the Capitalist State', *Annual Review of Sociology* 7, 1981, pp. 1–27.

9. Detailed statistics available at www.ukpublicspending.co.uk.

10. The ability to make such calculations is what is generally esteemed as 'pragmatism', and is esteemed highly in the British civil service. See Chapter 3.

Given that these compromises can always be revoked, reorganised, or shifted in favour of one side or other, there is in fact no *necessary* reason why the costs of a democratic state will tend to be pushed higher than can be covered with revenues. The historical experience of neoliberalism suggests that any upward pressure on spending imposed by legitimation functions is at least partially contingent on political struggles – a politically mobilised business community in alliance with the Right can force down popular expectations.

This helps place the conflict between democracy and capitalism, which O'Connor highlighted in explaining the 'fiscal crisis', in its true perspective. Of course capitalist democracy is not simply a deceit, but it is a highly ambiguous or 'contradictory' form of social organisation. Democracy is an inherently collectivist and egalitarian type of activity; capitalism is anything but. Democratic *ends* are also often collectivist and egalitarian to the point where they conflict with capitalist ends. The attempt by the state to organise class hegemony in a democratic context can result in social compromises which cost more in terms of revenue than the capitalist economy is able to supply without suffering serious dysfunctions. Today's austerity offensives can be seen as an attempt to revoke and reorganise certain of these compromises to the advantage of the ruling class, while modifying the institutional structure in which they were embedded. This necessarily implies conflict, and it implies a continued attempt to limit the democratic aspects of the state, whether by privatisation or authoritarian legislation.

This conflict, and the need for capital to *rein in* democracy while retaining its basic institutional format, is recognised in key neoliberal texts and forms the basis for a great deal of neoliberal praxis. It partially accounts for the escalated authoritarianism of, not just austerity regimes, but neoliberal statecraft in general. And this is where a second, related crisis is invoked. That of 'ungovernability'.

The inadequacy of state capacity in the face of social dysfunction was, of course, a key theme of the Right in the 1970s – whether it was racialised 'mugging' panics, or axe-grinding about strikes and protests, there was a general sensation that people were no longer doing as they were told. But the concept of 'ungovernability' became popular on both Left and Right, and was linked connotatively to a series of setbacks for capitalist democracies – the end of the 'golden age' of capitalist growth, the oil shocks, crime waves, the reverberations of 1968 and the spread of industrial militancy.[11] The diagnosis of a 'crisis of governability' culminated most notoriously in the Trilateral Commission report[12] which characterised the crisis as one arising from an 'excess of democracy'. What was meant by this was that too much popular participation overloaded bureaucratic states with 'demands' and agendas which they struggled to accommodate or synthesise in a viable way. States would thus struggle to pass effective laws or provide services, and would lose authority as a result. The increased activity of the government had decreased its authority: the more it did, the less it was obeyed. The recommended solution was to beef up the authority of central government and roll back popular participation: so much for the neoliberal fairy tale about getting government off our backs; far more the trend is for the government to get *us* off *its* back.

This was in essence remarkably similar to the critique of over-active bureaucrats coming from neoliberals and 'public choice' theorists. Friedrich Hayek, in his later work, had lamented the weakening of the state by its democratic entanglements – echoing elements of the critique of the party-political state made by Carl Schmitt. Public choice theorists argued the same essential point in a different way, maintaining that the involvement of the state in servicing various constituencies entangled it in a tight mesh of interest groups which drove up costs and incentivised bureaucratic inefficiency. The concept of 'ungovernability' thus implies that governments ought not to become entangled in managing the social needs of various constituencies and that the appropriate response is either

---

11. See Clause Offe, 'Ungovernability', in Stephan A. Jansen, Eckhard Schroter and Nico Stehr, eds., *Fragile Stabilität – stabile Fragilität*, Springer, Berlin, 2013, pp. 77–87.

12. Michael J. Crozier, Samuel P. Huntington and Joji Watanuki, *The Crisis of Democracy: Report on the Governability of Democracies to the Trilateral Commission*, New York University Press, New York, 1975. The commission was a think-tank of sorts established by liberal capitalists and intellectuals such as David Rockefeller and Zbigniew Brzezinski. The Report can be accessed at www.trilateral.org.

to moderate those demands through institutional accommodation (the social democratic response) or to confront and punish them (the neoliberal response).[13] In this sense, the notion of a 'crisis of governability' was part of a general turn to authoritarianism and counter-democratic politics.

The *moral* authoritarianism at the heart of austerity resonates in this purview.[14] For as much as austerity is justified by supposed harsh necessity (the 'fiscal crisis'), it is necessarily edged with punitive normative assumptions. A basic assumption of austerity is that economic efficiency is incompatible with egalitarianism. 'Efficiency' means allocating resources in such a way as to encourage 'enterprise' and thus growth. That means a diverse array of material incentives for businesses, such as tax cuts, regulatory changes, investment opportunities in public services and so on. It can also mean incentivising entrepreneurial behaviour on the part of individuals, such as house buying. Spending scarce resources on income support, housing benefits or other services for the poor is clearly not apt to encourage 'enterprise'. On the contrary, the assumption is that it encourages idleness and a 'culture of dependency'. As such, in a period of greater scarcity than usual, austerians argue that resources should be shifted as much as possible away from consumption and toward 'investment'.[15] Simultaneously, those whose purported lack of enterprise has led to their imposing a crippling burden upon the state must be punitively dealt with, coercively removed from the state's teat and given 'incentives' to embrace the joys of entrepreneurialism.

The concept of 'ungovernability' is thus useful in so far as it establishes clearly the ideological connection between austerity and the drift toward authoritarianism. However, a superior conceptual

---

13. See Offe, 'Ungovernability'.
14. On this, see Martha McCluskey, 'Law and Economic Austerity', *Classcrits*, 17 November 2010.
15. This is very much the approach of mandarin British austerians such as Mervyn King, who as Governor of the Bank of England argued emphatically that the economy had to be rebalanced away from private and public consumption. See Richard Seymour, 'Why the British Elite Insist on More Austerity (it's not that they're stupid)', *The Guardian*, 27 November 2012.

beginning, as Stuart Hall suggested in the context of Britain's crisis of the '70s, is the Gramscian notion of a 'crisis of authority'.[16] This involves the breakdown on multiple levels of the organisation of hegemony. Consent to the goals of the power bloc evaporates, and the intellectual, moral, scientific and institutional resources of hegemony are depleted. The ruling class 'has failed in some major political undertaking', 'huge masses ... have passed suddenly from a state of political passivity to a certain activity ... this is precisely the crisis of hegemony, or general crisis of the State'.[17]

A full-blown 'crisis of authority' is, in fact, a potentially revolutionary moment – and such instances are rare in core capitalist democracies. The British capitalist state, in particular, has rarely had to fight for its life: it has not suffered revolution, invasion, occupation or defeat to a militarily superior rival for centuries. Its colonial losses were considerable, and the source of much axe-grinding on the Right, but were managed without much disrupting the continuity of the state. If, moreover, Britain lost its colonial possessions, it did not entirely lose its imperialist dominance, with considerable global advantages. It benefits from EU membership without being entangled in the Eurozone, and thus has far more independence of action than, say, Greece or Spain. It has a globally powerful financial sector, and the Bank of England has been able to print money to stimulate lending throughout the economic downturn.

Nonetheless, the concept of a crisis of authority remains a good criterion of historical analysis against which to judge the political crises afflicting states. In the UK, the general upsurge of strikes and social disobedience in the 1970s seemed at times to exceed the state's capacity for dealing with them; that has not happened in this crisis, despite some sporadic struggles. The question is why not, and what has happened to those sudden passages 'from a state of political passivity to one of a certain activity'?

---

16. Stuart Hall, Chas Critcher, Tony Jefferson, John Clarke and Brian Roberts, *Policing the Crisis: Mugging, the State, and Law and Order*, Macmillan, London, 1978, pp. 216–17.

17. Gramsci, *Selections from the Prison Notebooks of Antonio Gramsci*, p. 210.

A popular left-wing response to this question is, essentially, 'All Cops Are Bastards': identifying direct physical repression not just as the dominant strategy of the state with respect to popular unrest or non-compliance in the neoliberal era, but as the necessary crisis response of austerity regimes. In one format, this idea relies on the old concept of the state as a 'machinery of repression', which hardly does justice to the complexity of modern states (of which more later). A more sophisticated analysis of policing under neoliberalism treats police as essentially the armed bureaucrats of neoliberal restructuring. Law and order policing, using 'zero tolerance' and anti-vagrancy laws, reinforces the dependency of the working class on market relations, and helps undermine collectivist recourses. Those among the poor who seek to survive and reproduce themselves outside of the wage form by one means or another are punished. This has 'little, if anything, to do with crime-fighting'.[18]

There is an element of truth in this type of analysis. It is manifestly the case that the decision as to what is socially costly behaviour, what shall be prohibited, and what shall be punished, is ideological. As Robert Reiner points out, neoliberalism produces many social evils which are not prohibited, though they could be. Meanwhile, aside from restrictions on collectivist activity such as trade union action, there is evidence of 'zero tolerance' policing and related techniques, backed by a barrage of central government directives and political pressure, being used to curtail non-waged survival mechanisms such as begging. And there is a long history of capitalist states using repression to acculturate people to market-dependency and work discipline.[19]

---

18. See, for instance, Todd Gordon, 'The Political Economy of Law-and-Order Policies: Policing, Class Struggle, and Neoliberal Restructuring', *Studies in Political Economy* 75, 2005, available at http://spe.library.utoronto.ca/index.php.

19. On 'zero tolerance' and neoliberalism, see Maurice Punch, *Zero Tolerance Policing*, The Policy Press, Bristol, 2007; and Robert Reiner, *Law and Order: An Honest Citizen's Guide to Crime and Control*, Polity Press, Cambridge, 2007, Chapter 1. On the history of capitalism and law, see Peter Linebaugh, *The London Hanged: Crime and Civil Society in the Eighteenth Century*, Verso, London and New York, 2006.

But the analysis is hamstrung by two key problems. First, it leaves us with the obvious question of what 'crime-fighting' is, if it does not include the police implementing strategies to uphold norms encoded in law; what crime is, if it is not behaviour which is ideologically proscribed. It seems to imply that there is, aside from this activity, another type of 'crime-fighting', more consistent with the image of the police as just another public service delivered by a municipal agency to serve a taxpaying community, and that law-and-order policing is a departure from this. Such is simply not consistent with the historical record.[20] Paul Gilroy reminds us that 'crime' is a profoundly ideological category, criminalisation a profoundly ideological process. This is linked to 'race' in so far as racist ideologies can help to justify the criminalisation of a particular type of contentious behaviour:

> In a 'law and order society', ideologies of illegality have a special pertinence, particularly when the legitimacy of police practice becomes more difficult to secure. Ideas of black criminality appear in the struggle for legitimation, intersect with racist common sense and, in that process, provide a wealth of justifications for illegitimate, discriminatory and of course illegal police practices at the grass roots level ... Police theorizations of 'alien blackness' as black criminality show where the filaments of racist ideology disappear into the material institutions of the capitalist state.[21]

Recognising this helps avoid the serious analytical mistake of counterposing 'real politics' to criminality, which becomes particularly important when the criminalisation of protest is such a salient part of the political terrain. The process of selective criminalisation is one that is intimately imbricated with the process of state recomposition.

Second, to treat law-and-order policing as simply the enforcement of a neoliberal and 'monetarist' accumulation strategy is to treat

---

20. For a trenchant critique of such notions, see Paul Gilroy and Joe Simm, 'Law, Order and the State of the Left', *Capital and Class* 9:1, 1985, pp. 15–55.
21. Paul Gilroy, 'Police and Thieves', in Stuart Hall et al., *The Empire Strikes Back: Race and Racism in 70s Britain*, Macmillan, London, 1982.

the state as a mere reflex of the economy. It is to ignore what the neoliberals themselves did not; that the state has its own relative autonomy, and that it plays a role in constructing the economy. It does not merely police the 'wage form', it helps create it. It constitutes it in various ways, legally structuring it. Some manifestations of the 'wage form' are proscribed. For example, the 'war on drugs' clearly penalises workers in the drugs trade as much as it does enterprising capitalists, by classifying their actions as criminal. The same point could be made of laws penalising sex workers. These are forms of cultural and moral regulation that are incapable of being explained if one does not give the state a certain 'relative autonomy' from the economy.

It is certainly true that the containment of social disorder arising from contested austerity measures necessitated increases in police numbers and an expansion of their powers. Mrs Thatcher's beefing up of police to cope with riots and then deal with the unions is a case in point. It is also true that the repressive apparatuses have expanded in the neoliberal period – the most compelling example being the growth of the penal system in the United States, as governments shifted resources from welfare to punishment. In the UK as well, police numbers have increased in the neoliberal era, and the prison population has climbed, particularly since the election of New Labour.[22] But while this certainly has consequences for the general

---

22. Thatcher increased police numbers from just shy of 110,000 to approximately 125,000. Under Major, police numbers remained relatively flat. Under New Labour, they increased from 125,051 in March 1997 to 141,631 in March 2010. See 'Police Service Strength, England and Wales: 31 March 1997 to 30 September 2000', House of Commons Library, Research Paper 01/28, 16 March 2001; and also 'Police Workforce, England and Wales: March 2011 supplementary tables', available at www.data.gov.uk. The prison population almost doubled from 44,386 in June 1993 to 86,048 in June 2012. In fairness, the prison population had been steadily rising for some time, but the growth very suddenly accelerated from the mid 1990s due to harsher penalties. See 'Story of the Prison Population 1993–2012', Ministry of Justice, March 2013, available at www.gov.uk; and Gavin Berman and Aliyah Dar, 'Prison Population Statistics', House of Commons, 29 July 2013, available at www.parliament.uk.

disciplining of populations,[23] it is part of a far more sophisticated series of responses than simple repression.

Consider the policing of protest. The convergence in the core capitalist states is not exclusively toward more repressive styles of crowd management, but rather toward a more differentiated approach. Police tend to prefer consensual and negotiated approaches when dealing with larger protests representing 'official' bodies, where they take a greater physical distance from the people whose activities they are managing. One is more likely to find coppers grumbling from the sidelines of trade union marches that 'we're public sector workers too' than one is to find them ladling out ultra-violence. By contrast, smaller groups of protesters representing loose social coalitions, campaign alliances and so on, are more likely to be deemed 'extremist', 'terrorist' or even – theatrical gasp – 'anarchist', and thus subject to militarised policing, direct surveillance and physical coercion, with the invocation of 'anti-terrorist' or other repressive legislation.[24]

Just as the definition of crime is necessarily ideological, the decision as to what constitutes an 'official' protest or an 'extremist' outrage is in part ideological and normative, deriving from the legal and political culture of policing in a given state and bureaucratic categories deployed by local forces.[25] This is a clear sense in which the dominant ideology – that which normalises the 'ontological and

---

23. See Wacquant, *Punishing the Poor: The Neoliberal Government of Social Insecurity*, and also Ruth Wilson Gilmore, *Golden Gulag: Prisons, Surplus, Crisis and Opposition in Globalizing California*, University of California Press, Berkeley CA, 2006.

24. For a detailed overview of the trends, see Donatella della Porta, Abby Peterson and Herbert Reiter, eds., *The Policing of Transnational Protest*, Asghgate, Farnham, 2006.

25. Relatively recent UK examples would include the characterisation of Occupy London as 'terrorist' and Bristol protest movements as 'extremists'. But this is a trend that has been visible in antiwar and anticapitalist protests for at least 15 years. See Shiv Malik, 'Occupy London's Anger Over Police "Terrorism" Document', *The Guardian*, 5 December 2011; Daniel Evans, 'Police Cracking Down on Bristol Rioters and Extremists', *The Bristol Post*, 13 September 2013.

epistemological premises of a particular and historical form of social order'[26] – is materialised in the practices of the state. The state's role in producing the social classifications which it then acts upon – crime, morality, nation, 'race', and so on – is as essential to it as its role in organising accumulation strategies. The moral and symbolic categories which emerge to explain crisis and social disorder also become the means, in the form of police practice, through which crisis and disorder are organised and managed. These categories help cleave the population into strategically manageable strata and sectors, allowing the appropriate police technologies to be deployed against a suitably limited target group.

Further, there is no necessary reason why the repressive apparatuses must *expand* in the context of austerity. I have suggested that the pressure to reduce the burden of state expenditures on taxes tends to increase just as the need for state intervention to regulate dysfunctions increases. When it comes to the management of populations, this presents a dilemma over what to do with policing budgets. In many cases, the political need to have a loyal police force trumps any spending cuts, and governments ring-fence police spending as a result. This has not been the case in the UK in recent years, where police forces have been compelled to cut their spending and their workforces, shedding 32,400 staff.[27]

This is in stark contrast to the qualitative expansion and upgrading of police budgets, numbers, and technological assets in the first wave of neoliberal austerity under Mrs Thatcher. What is happening here is that the police are being reorganised like every other public bureaucracy on the basis of ideas laid out by public choice theorists. The current Metropolitan Police Commissioner Bernard Hogan-Howe maintains that the police are like every public monopoly in having no competition, and therefore must be reformed to simulate the basic structures of competitive markets within

26. Philip Corrigan and Derek Sayer, *The Great Arch: English State Formation as a Cultural Revolution*, Basil Blackwell, Oxford, 1985, p. 5.

27. For a detailed report on the implementation of police cuts, see 'Policing in Austerity: One Year On', Her Majesty's Inspectorate of the Constabulary, July 2012, available at www.hmic.gov.uk.

themselves. This, it is thought, will stimulate better performance and innovation; technological and military-style solutions, combined with certain techniques borrowed from behavioural economics, will make up for the loss of man-power.[28]

This is linked to a series of reforms being implemented by the Cameron administration, such as abolishing police authorities based on civil society 'representation', and replacing them with elected commissioners based on the US model of populist law-and-order policing. This is primarily about how the legitimacy of policing is secured: politically moderate oversight from civil society figures and mainstream politicians is essentially being replaced by a model of legitimacy based on 'celebrity cops'. That these reforms are rejected by a significant sector of the police establishment represented by the likes of Sir Hugh Orde or Sir Paul Stephenson[29] is indicative of how thorough the recomposition of the state apparatuses really is. The implementation of public choice theory in the police bureaucracies alongside serious spending cuts is a novelty. But it is the use of this process to implement a new technology of policing – a new ensemble of techniques linked to a new legal and political culture within which policing happens – that is important here. 'Total policing' may well involve a more confrontational and directly politicised approach to the management of 'extremists' and other subaltern groups.[30] This has certainly been the experience of protesters in the UK, for example. But overall it is likely to involve a more *sophisticated* and *discriminating* deployment of resources.

This should not be read as implying omnipotence on the part of police agencies. They are bureaucracies whose actions are

28. Bernard Hogan-Howe, 'Total Policing: The Future of Policing in London', address to the London School of Economics, 16 January 2012, available at www.lse.ac.uk.

29. See Policing: Police and Crime Commissioners, HC 511, Second Report of Session 2010–11 – Report, Together with Formal Minutes, Oral and Written Evidence, House of Commons – Home Affairs Committee, The Stationery Office, 2010.

30. See Liz Fekete, 'Total Policing: Reflections From the Frontline', *Race and Class* 54, January–March 2013.

determined within a matrix of institutional pressures and conflicts, and which must – since they aim to police 'by consent' – register public discontent. Even carefully targeted, ideologically coded coercion can generate crises of consent. Their ideological appeals – that they must prevent 'extremists' and 'anarchists' from breaching the peace, for example – do not always gain acceptance. The use of 'kettling' and militarised policing against protesters in the UK, beginning with Reclaim the Streets protesters in the 1990s, has produced a significant backlash. This was particularly the case after the killing of Ian Tomlinson amid a typically violent police response to G20 protests in 2009. This resulted in legal struggles and unwelcome court verdicts,[31] and a consequent partial retreat from such methods. The surprise success of student protesters in taking over the Conservative Party headquarters in November 2010 resulted in tremendous institutional pressure from the government and a grovelling apology from the Metropolitan Police Commissioner. Police then responded to future student protests with a greatly escalated form of the repressive policing, the legitimacy of which was in this case upheld by the courts.[32]

There are also the effects of wider political conflicts which can undermine the legitimacy of police and disrupt its organisational coherence for a certain period. The police represent themselves as being 'at the interface' of political struggle rather than participants. When the politicised nature of policing, ordinarily submerged beneath 'common sense' assumptions, is rendered obvious, the ordinary means by which the police process social conflict and secure legitimacy are undermined. The England riots of 2011 were preceded by a profound crisis for the police as senior officers were swept up in the 'Hackgate' scandal. The latter involved deep-seated corruption on the part of the Murdoch press, as well as the police and politicians with whom News Corporation employees consorted and bribed. There

---

31. Vikram Dodd, 'Thousands May Sue Over Police Kettling at G20 Protests', *The Guardian*, 14 April 2011; 'Kettle Police Acted Unlawfully at Rally, High Court Rules', *BBC News online*, 18 June 2013.

32. Shiv Malik, 'Teenage Protesters Lose Case Against Kettling', *The Guardian*, 8 September 2011.

was not just corruption, but a record of collusion between different sectors of the British establishment; the nexus of the police, the Murdoch press and the Conservative Party having been consolidated during the anti-union offensives of the 1980s. The resulting losses to the police force included the resignations of Metropolitan Police Commissioner Sir Paul Stephenson and his assistant commissioner John Yates. This disarray formed the backdrop to the police killing of Mark Duggan in Tottenham, and their response to the ensuing riots – during which it was clear for a time that they lacked the capacity to cope. The existence of active consent in this context, and indeed the willingness of certain groups to substitute for the police, eventually allowed the police to recoup their control of the streets.[33]

The point here is that while it is true that the techniques of state dominance have shifted decisively in an authoritarian direction in the neoliberal era, even this has a necessary ideological dimension; even this requires consent, or at least acquiescence. The police should certainly not be interpreted as 'weak' by any means, but their strategies for containing challenges to the status quo are effective as much because their legitimacy is widely accepted, because their coercion is understood to be fair and appropriate by a viable majority of people, as because they successfully brutalise target audiences. Most people, for most of the time, appear to be willing to defer to the police and courts to the extent that they self-regulate; they internalise the discipline of the law and become its agents.[34] As importantly, the opposition forces with which police have to contend are weak, incoherent, and their organisations transient. This weakness – the absence of any sustainable counter-hegemonic alliance, and the

---

33. The aftermath of the riots produced complex effects on the legitimacy of the police – hardening support for cops among some, hardening opposition among others. See Katrin Hohl, Betsy Stanko and Tim Newburn, 'The Effect of the 2011 London Disorder on Public Opinion of Police and Attitudes Towards Crime, Disorder, and Sentencing', *Policing* 7:3, September 2013.

34. See Jonathan Jackson, Ben Bradford, Betsy Stanko and Katrin Hohl, *Just Authority? Trust in the Police in England and Wales*, Routledge, London, 2012.

acquiescence of politically passive and unorganised masses – allows the redeployment of legal-police networks to function with far less friction than it might.

The way in which I have tried to account for these two political crises and their unfolding implies, but does not articulate, a particular conception of state power. Having rejected the notion of the state as simply a 'machinery of repression', I have nonetheless identified the state as organising 'class hegemony' through a series of continually negotiated compromises between the dominant and the dominated. Why should the state do all this? What exactly is the state anyway?

The Mystery of the Neoliberal State

The state, as suggested above, is central to the implementation of austerity as part of a growth strategy for capitalism. The problem with discussing 'the state', however, is that no such *thing* exists. This may not be what you want to hear in the context of a polemic against austerity, but just imagine I'm Lawrence Fishburne and I'm telling you: *the state is an illusion.* Of course, in a way, we know this. We know 'the state' isn't a tangible object like a carbon steel baton. But there is always a temptation to reify it, to talk about it as if it is actually a thing – a thing that can be used as an 'instrument', or 'smashed'. Taking such an approach, it would be hard to see how states could be the site of constant antagonism, struggle and flux, as they manifestly are. In order to understand how neoliberal practices transformed capitalist states, it is necessary to really get behind the concept of 'the state'.[35]

In one sense, it seems as if 'the state' is just a social category – we talk about 'the state' in reference to an array of disparate phenomena we experience, from a prison to a hospital to a parking ticket. All

---

35. The following analysis draws pretty heavily from Poulantzas, *State, Power, Socialism*; Nicos Poulantzas, *Political Power and Social Classes*, Verso, London, 1978; and especially a useful essay by Peter Bratsis, 'Unthinking the State: Reification, ideology and the State as a Social Fact', in Stanley Aaronowitz and Peter Bratsis, eds., *Paradigm Lost: State Theory Reconsidered*, University of Minnesota Press, Minneapolis and London, 2002.

of these things, we are told, are somehow part of 'the state', even though the only thing that seems to connect them is the fact that they are classified as such. Moreover, the distinction between what is and what is not part of the state – the distinction between public and private spheres – is itself a politico-legal artifice, a product of the institutions of 'the state'. In this light, it would seem that 'the state' is simply not real; it is at best a convenient fiction, at worst a superstition that reinforces political domination by mystifying its mechanisms. Corrigan and Sayer suggest that the state is a cultural form involved in 'moral regulation':

[a] project of normalizing, rendering natural, taken for granted, in a word 'obvious', what are in fact ontological and epistemo-logical premises of a particular and historical form of social order ... Centrally, state agencies attempt to give unitary and unifying expression to what are in reality multifaceted and differential historical experiences of groups within society, denying their particularity.[36]

Clearly, however, that can only take us so far. The institutions of 'the state' are obviously real enough, even if they are not 'things'. And these institutions possess a certain *centralised, hierarchical unity*.[37] This means there is at least a socially produced reality behind the state idea. The point, though, is that this reality – these institutions and their unity – should be treated as a historical outcome which needs to be explained, rather than as something to be taken for granted.

This is where Nicos Poulantzas made a significant breakthrough in state theory, by arguing that the state is a *social relation*. As he

36. Philip Corrigan and Derek Sayer, *The Great Arch: English State Formation as a Cultural Revolution*, Basil Blackwell, Oxford, 1985, p. 5.

37. However fissiparous these institutions and personnel may be in daily practice, their formal structural unity is sustained by the dominance of one or more branches or apparatuses of the state – typically the executive – over the others. In principle, the information flows upward, toward the centre, so that there can be an attempt by the state leadership to surveil and control its apparatuses. Likewise, the command flows downward and outward.

put it, the state is 'a relationship of forces, or more precisely the material condensation of such a relationship'.[38] What does this mean? An example will perhaps explain it. Robin Blackburn, discussing Hanoverian Britain in his classic book *The Overthrow of Colonial Slavery*, describes the political settlement in England after the 'Glorious Revolution' of 1688 and the installation of William of Orange as king.[39] The new political arrangements favoured the direct rule of the newly dominant capitalist class. A monarch with weak legitimacy allowed the propertied oligarchy to be assertive of its interests in parliament, while dominating most state posts at local as well as national level – as County Commissioners, Lords Lieutenant, or Justices of the Peace, as well as MPs. Highly lucrative public offices – such as in the Bank of England and chartered companies – were held as private property. As statesmen, they established corporations; as corporate members, they profited from the enterprise. As MPs they legislated; as Justices of the Peace they interpreted the law. So, the English state, having been a feudal regime, became a capitalist one.

This didn't happen instantaneously. It had taken a couple of centuries for the English capitalist class to develop and accumulate its wealth, to become a political power, to fight for its interests, and finally bid for control of the state by the overthrow and regicide of King Charles II. Moreover, it wasn't a simple case of one class speaking directly, univocally, through the leadership of the Roundheads. In order to defeat the old elites – nobles, the old merchant class – an emerging capitalist class comprising landowners and new merchants

---

38. Poulantzas' conception has been criticised for 'class-reductionism', inasmuch as he focuses exclusively on the balance of *class* forces in determining the form of the state, but his analysis can be extended to include the effects of struggles other than class – over gender, race, nationality, etc. – so that, in other words, the state is seen as the material condensation of the balance of political forces in toto. See Alexander Gallas, Lars Bretthauer, John Kannankulam and Ingo Stützle, eds., *Reading Poulantzas*, Merlin Press, Pontypool, 2011; also, Bob Jessop and Nicos Poulantzas, *Marxist Theory and Political Strategy*, Macmillan, London, 1985.

39. Robin Blackburn, *The Overthrow of Colonial Slavery*, Verso, London and New York, 1988, pp. 69–77.

with links to the colonies, had to assemble the support of some of the labouring classes, and it had to temporarily arouse a broad, complex political coalition with a significant far left. Having achieved power, it then had to contain and suppress the labouring classes. Eventually, in 1688, it reached an historic compromise with a weakened feudal nobility to consolidate its political domination.

The system that arose, with its narrow franchise and rotten boroughs, represented capitalist rule at its earliest stage. Through centuries of struggle, and adaptation, the state would incorporate wider layers of the population. It accepted a franchise for the middle class, then for working class men, then for women. It incorporated popular demands for welfare and redistribution, eventually institutionalised in the post-Second World War social democratic state. But the major offices of the state, its laws, its apparatuses and its divisions of labour have continued to be elaborated under capitalist domination.

This gives us a concrete example of how a particular state form arises out of a complex political class struggle, how it comes to condense within its material institutions the balance of political forces in the wider society, and how its apparatuses and personnel continue to respond to ongoing struggles and adapt to new relations of forces. Its attempt to organise and process social and political antagonisms results in a complex internal articulation of the relations present in society as a whole. But it isn't infinitely malleable, nor is it just a screenshot of the balance of forces at a given historical moment. It is the result of the *accumulated outcomes of past political struggles*, concentrated in a particular institutional format. As such its form, its materiality, its language, are heavily pre-structured in favour of the class that has traditionally dominated it. It remains 'impregnated' (in Goran Therborn's phrase[40]) with the goals of a particular social class, the capitalist class, allowing that class to rule politically even if it doesn't directly occupy the dominant apparatuses. This is the difficulty that left-wing parties face upon assuming office – the institutions are weighted against their project, the policy language they must use geared toward reproducing the existing order, the existing state personnel resistant to radical change.

40. Therborn, *What Does the Ruling Class Do When It Rules?*

There is more to it than this, however. It isn't good enough just to say that the capitalist class rules politically. One of the most salient features of this class is that its members are constantly at each other's throats, in brutal competition with one another. Moreover, the general interests of one fraction of capital (say, finance) may not be the same as another (say, agriculture). And if ongoing political struggles are condensed within the state, then this competitive struggle between different capitals and fractions of capital is also likely to find expression there in various ways. So, for Poulantzas, the state is a field of struggle, in which the relations between different classes, fractions of classes, and strata, are politically condensed, and vie with one another for control. Effective control is exercised by a *power bloc*, representing not one class but several class fractions under the hegemony of one particular fraction which provides leadership to the whole by incorporating their interests in its mode of rule.[41]

What one would expect, then, is that power blocs would be formed, deformed, and reformed, relative to the state of power within society at any given juncture. A new phase in the development of capitalist civilisation, based on a new relationship of forces, would lead to the formation of a new power bloc and a new configuration of state power. This relational approach can help us to understand what is novel about the neoliberal state, why it is different from previous forms, while remaining a capitalist state.

The Neoliberal Power Bloc in Crisis

How is a state recomposed? How is a new power bloc formed? It is not a matter of changing personnel. As indicated in the last chapter, at each phase of capitalist development a new configuration of

---

41. I stress that this is all very indirect for Poulantzas. It is not a question of direct representatives being delegated by the investment and merchant banks to work in the state, or of lobbying, or of political donations – though these things happen. It is rather a matter of their considerable power within society – society's dependence on them for its effective reproduction, translating into an attempt by state personnel to look after their interests, while also responding to demands from less powerful groups.

power emerges based on a particular strategy for growth. It is the reorganisation of the state apparatuses, and the institutionalisation of new practices and rituals to meet this new strategy, which signals that a new power bloc has emerged.

And as I also suggested in Chapter 1, the course of the present crisis and its management by states gives us some indication as to what sort of power bloc is in charge, and how it will adapt. In the first instance, the US state took the lead in fire-fighting and implementing long-term adjustments to cope with the failure. This reflected both the *financialisation* of the state (as financial capital has increased its dominance), the increasing centrality of its monetary and financial responsibilities in the neoliberal era, and its *internationalisation* (as US capital has internationalised).

The US had been central to combating previous global crises, largely because the American state had already, through its assiduous role in constructing the institutions of global capitalism, inter-nationalised. It had extended its influence in allied states through post-war aid and reconstruction, as well as through the global financial architecture and military apparatuses it developed. It had acted to co-opt and discipline de-colonising societies, and used debt and financial crises to restructure Third World states in particular, and integrate them into the US sphere of dominance. Decades of neoliberal institutionalisation and 'free trade' agreements had been initiated by the United States. This was critical in allowing global chains of production to emerge, centred on US capital. Apple, for example, based in California, could source labour and materials in South East Asia, its products finally readied in China, to sell to markets in North America and Europe, and retain the largest share of the revenue.[42]

As such, with its clout centred on Wall Street and the Treasury, and its interest in protecting the world system, there was no agency other than the US which was capable of taking a lead in resolving this crisis. The means by which it did so were: 1) establish a working group to coordinate policy responses and coordination with financial

---

42. This example is provided by Panitch and Gindin in *The Making of Global Capitalism*, p. 287.

regulators such as the Securities Exchange Commission; 2) assemble a consortium of banks and financial organisations to take measures to stabilize the system, based loosely on the model of the bailout of Long Term Capital Management; 3) keeping liquidity in the world monetary system going by having the Federal Reserve provide dollars to the world's central banks as well as to Wall Street; 4) nationalise the Federal National Mortgage Association, and the Federal Home Loan Mortgage Corporation, to assure international investors that they would not default on their debts; 5) begin to reform the regulation of the banks with more powers for the Federal Reserve; 6) finally, when private sector bailouts failed to materialise, and Lehman Brothers went down, organise a gargantuan public sector bailout worth an initial $700 billion, via the Treasury.

The coordinates of this plan are consistent with the long-term financialisation of the state. They entrenched and deepened the authority of the Fed and the Treasury within the state, so that they could act as guarantors of capitalism with a particular eye to protecting US financial dominance. The mutual interpenetration of the state and finance capital, characteristic of the neoliberal era, was deepened as the state acted to assume as much of the risk of investment as possible, while allowing private investors to collect the rewards.[43]

This resolution did not necessarily entail an austerity shock. The Obama administration, as suggested in the introduction, has been quite content to use limited stimulus spending, followed by limited retrenchment. Faithful to neoliberal orthodoxy, it has at most enacted the 'permanent austerity' that neoliberal states have adopted – a permanent strait-jacket on spending and borrowing. In this pursuit, it has implemented spending cuts which are not qualitatively different from those of the Clinton administration. The Federal Reserve has expressed its preference for no serious fiscal contraction, at least for the present.[44] It is at the level of local state administrations that austerity has been pursued, under pressure from

43. Albo, Gindin and Panitch, *In and Out of Crisis*, pp. 63–8.
44. Binyamin Appelbaum, 'In Surprise, Fed Decides to Maintain Pace of Stimulus', *New York Times*, 18 September 2013.

some local business elites and a layer of the middle class.[45] Notable, for example, has been the record drop in public sector employment during Obama's administration. This has overwhelmingly been the result of state-level redundancies rather than federal action,[46] and has been most vigorously prosecuted by Republican hit men with the backing of medium-to-large businesses most determined to cut wages and tax bills. This caution on the part of liberal state managers is undoubtedly related to the internationalisation of the American state, to the extent that it has responsibilities regarding its global dominance (providing China with an export market, for example), and simultaneously has the advantage of being able to sustain a much higher level of borrowing than other states. It also has to do with the need to maintain the great achievement of neoliberalism, which is the incorporation of the mass of the population into the financial system. The devaluation of working class assets as a consequence of the crisis is a setback that any systematic austerity shock threatens to drastically worsen. Put briefly, the divisions among elites over whether to proceed with austerity reflects both the risks of the project and divergences of short-term interest.

The responses in other core capitalist states reflected a similar trend toward the elevation of central banks and treasuries, the protection of financial interests above all, and the interpenetration of state and capital. In the UK, for example, bailouts were organised through the Treasury, and liquidity preserved by the Bank of England, while nationalised banks were kept operating on a commercial basis 'at arm's length' from the government and with no direct oversight. In the EU, the power of finance ministers, the European Central Bank, and the International Monetary Fund in imposing structural adjustment, with the connivance of local states, has become legendary.

---

45. For an insight into the Tea Party's roots in provincial elites, see Michael Lind, 'Tea Party Radicalism is Misunderstood: Meet the "Newest Right"', *Salon*, 6 October 2013.

46. Dominic Rushe, 'Public Sector Cuts Dragging Down US's Already Fragile Economic Recovery', *The Guardian*, 31 May 2012.

Taken together with the austerity packages to which they are logically linked, the bailouts and ersatz 'nationalisations' reflect not so much a renewed vigour of state intervention as a redeployed state intervention more explicitly on the side of financial capital. They indicate the presence of a power bloc dominated by finance capital, which fraction appears to be increasing its dominance while entrenching its preferred accumulation strategies.

This can be illuminated by a thumbnail sketch of the shift from the post-war Keynesian system to the neoliberal system. In the post-war era, the dominant accumulation strategy was that sustained by the larger and more advanced sectors of industry. Heavy manufacturing had displaced the traditional coalition of financial capital, mining capital (coal and steel) and, in the UK, colonial capital. These manufacturers were capital-intensive and enjoyed high profit margins, sufficient to make certain concessions to the working class regarding wage growth and tax-funded services. They were also dependent on a relatively large number of skilled workers and required a degree of social harmony to ensure predictability in production. As a result, a social compromise between capital and labour based critically on a recognition and institutionalisation of union power suited the dominant production methods. The state would support industry with subsidies and wage controls, and sustain nationalised businesses under the management of personnel drawn from private capital. It would support demand to a limited degree and provide a healthy, educated workforce. And it would help coordinate investment to ensure British global competitiveness. This strategy began to suffer setbacks during the 1960s due to increasing international competition, the loss of the colonial empire and related export markets, and the strains of an expanded welfare state. As a result, governments abandoned several aspects of the compromise and began to try to curtail union power and liberalise markets.[47]

---

47. On the post-war power bloc, see Henk Overbeek, 'Financial Capital and the Crisis in Britain', *Capital and Class* 4, 1980; on the early attempts to break with the consensus, see Robin Blackburn, 'The Heath Government: A New Course for British Capitalism', *New Left Review* I/70, November–December 1970.

The 'fiscal crisis' of the 1970s provided the terrain in which a coalition of ruling class interests, informed by neoliberal praxis, intervened and began to mould a new accumulation strategy. The crisis it responded to was the result of many factors – above all the declining growth and profitability of the core capitalist economies, and the inability of the old power bloc to effectively suppress wage claims or cut spending. We have seen that in the context of the New York City fiscal crisis, financial capital largely succeeded in taking hold of the situation and forming the leadership of a new power bloc. It did this by interpreting the crisis as a result of state overspend imposed by militant unions and 'special interests', and then in shifting the balance of political forces within the state in their favour in order to manage an austerity-based solution. Similar methods were subsequently rolled out nationwide in the US.

The neoliberal power bloc that emerged represented the fruition of two key dynamics in the post-war period: the expansion of capital, and the internationalisation of capital. The basis for corporatism had been that the larger, nationally based manufacturing corporations had enjoyed a certain protection from competition and were able to plan for long-term growth in tandem with the state. But the growing scale and internationalisation of capitalist enterprises meant that nationally based corporations were increasingly in the position that small businesses had been for much of the post-war era. They were subject to vigorous competition and easily edged out of market by far larger transnational rivals. They experienced the state less as an ally in planning long-term profitable futures and more as burdensome and interfering. As a result, they began to shift in favour of growth strategies predicated on the abandonment of corporatism and the liberalisation of markets that had been developed intellectually by neoliberals and long supported by the large banks.[48]

The crucial stage in the emergence of a new power bloc was the imposition of a period of austerity, both in the United Kingdom and the United States. In the US, austerity involved a wide-ranging

---

48. Usefully discussed by Neil Davidson in 'The Neoliberal Era in Britain: Historical Developments and Current Perspectives', *International Socialism*, 139, Summer 2013.

programme of cuts and privatisations, but most saliently took the form of the so-called 'Volcker shock' in 1981. Federal Reserve Chairman Paul Volcker had become an extremely prominent figure in the American state by the late 1970s. He had played a critical role as a Treasury bureaucrat in the Nixon administration's abrupt changes to the international monetary system, which in their turn generated an explosion of new financial devices and streams of money-capital. This made it extremely important what the Federal Reserve did with interest rates. As Panitch and Gindin put it:

> It was highly significant that, in the new age of finance, the Federal Reserve came into much greater prominence. As a Fed paper later exulted: 'In the early '60s, the Federal Reserve was little known outside the financial services industry and university economics departments. Twenty years later Fed Chairman Paul Volcker was one of the most recognized names in American public life.' In fact, not only investors on Wall Street but businessmen everywhere increasingly seemed more attuned to the decisions of the Federal Reserve than Soviet managers were to Gosplan's ... The Fed 'increasingly became the fulcrum on which the US economy turned'.[49]

The 'shock' named after Volcker was a blunt restriction on the growth of the money supply, causing interest rates to soar, driving down the standard of living, driving down inflation, and – by means of the effects on employment – breaking the power of organised labour. One of the most significant results of this from the perspective of state institutions was its signalling of a concerted anti-inflationary commitment that secured the role of the Fed as the 'global anchor of a dollar-based world economy'. It stabilised the world monetary system without requiring the imposition of capital controls, which would necessarily require international coordination between states and would tend to strengthen the hand of the social democratic Left by giving governments more potential power for regulation

---

49. Panitch and Gindin, *The Making of Global Capitalism*, p. 177.

and intervention.[50] As suggested in Chapter 1, this shift to militant counter-inflation as the centre-piece of state economic strategy institutionalised the class objectives of finance capital.

Although the Republican Party was the major agency through which this shift was effected, the defeat of the Left and the unions throughout this process eased the process by which the Democratic Party would become a more impeccably neoliberal party in office than even the GOP. The neoliberal power bloc thus came to comprise the leaderships of the two dominant parties, the upper strata of the capitalist and managerial classes embedded in the larger manufacturing and service corporations, and above all Wall Street.

Mrs Thatcher's austerity programme was similarly based on a monetary and fiscal contraction, the better to attack inflation. Spending as a whole was cut by the government, aiming to reduce the public-sector borrowing requirement – but this was not simply a cuts package to 'balance the budget'. In so far as spending was to come down, it was because high expenditures were seen as the cause of Britain's economic backwardness, and therefore the idea was to make them as permanent as possible. But the government, far from simply cutting, deployed a series of material incentives and signals reflecting new priorities: taxes on consumption were raised, for example, while taxes on investment were decreased. Lay-offs and restructuring in the public sector were intended as much to weaken the unions and increase workers' dependence on markets as to save money. The government maintained the squeeze throughout the recession – concurrently embarking on a wide-ranging 'public order' crackdown, as its policies generated the predictable social eruptions.[51]

If Mrs Thatcher's leadership was defined by conflict – with the unions, the Left, the IRA – it would never be frictionless for business. The emergence and consolidation of a new power bloc in the British case took time, and required an attack on some practices favoured by sections of capital. One of the effects of austerity was to force through

---

50. See Panitch and Konings, eds., *American Empire and the Political Economy of Global Finance*, pp. 30–7.
51. See Andrew Gamble, *The Free Economy and the Strong State: The Politics of Thatcherism*, 2nd Edition, Palgrave Macmillan, London, 1988, pp. 107–19.

a purge of 'unproductive' manufacturing capital in the interests of a more 'competitive' British capitalism. This would dissolve a great deal of the material foundation for trade unionism while also destroying excess productive capacity, but it also threatened British capitalism's future growth prospects. Thatcher's government dropped wage controls, which had been an important tool for business in attempting to moderate union demands. They cut public spending at a time of recession, creating social unrest, when businesses might have preferred a degree of social harmony. The Thatcherites also took on their foes inside the Conservative Party and civil service elites, and began to reorganise the state apparatuses, bringing in business consultants and others to put the doctrines of neoliberal 'public choice' theorists to work. The involvement of sympathetic businesses in this was not coincidental: the neoliberal era would witness a growing fusion between state and private capital, with public-private partnerships their institutional trademark.

In any other circumstance, the destruction of manufacturing, the politically risky spending cuts, and the ditching of wage controls might have been resisted by business. But the fear of the Labour Left and militant trade unionism consolidated elite support for Thatcher, and her Falklands victory helped consolidate her position within her party leadership against those advocating alternative growth strategies. In later years, after the austerity shock, Thatcher would directly empower the financial sector with a new regulatory system aimed at easing transactions, while simultaneously breaking the 'big battalions' of organised labour, one after the other. The overall effect was to shift the balance of forces within the state away from trade union and popular constituencies and toward the banks and large capitalist enterprises. Eventually her successes against the Left and the unions ensured that the opposition Labour Party began to embrace her policies.[52] The neoliberal power bloc thus came to comprise the leaderships of the two dominant parties, the upper strata of the capitalist and managerial classes embedded in the larger

---

52. Arguably, the 'winter of discontent' was a pivotal moment in shifting elite opinion in favour of Thatcherism. See Colin Hay, 'Chronicles of a Death Foretold: The Winter of Discontent and Construction of the Crisis of British Keynesianism', *Parliamentary Affairs* 63:3, 2010, pp. 446–70; and

manufacturing and service corporations, and above all the City of London.[53]

This was the power bloc that can be said to have prevailed prior to the 2007 credit crunch with, as indicated in Chapter 1, some considerable successes. Its success in taking control of the policy response to the credit crunch and ensuing recessions is indicative of its continued power and the utter paucity of initiative, organisation and coherence on the part of its opponents. While some leftists had expected an old divide to open up between finance and manufacturing, with manufacturers pressing for a more Keynesian remedy based on support for employment and demand management, finance has retained its dominance. Were it even likely to be challenged in any serious way, the mechanism of bailouts and austerity ensured that such a challenge was foreclosed. Austerity can thus be interpreted, in this light, as a crisis response that expedites the recomposition of the state under the dominance of finance.

Example 3: The Eurozone, Greece and 'Failed States'

Like 'sex' and 'violence', the words 'Europe' and 'crisis' seem to have been in near constant conjunction in recent years. The stakes have

---

on the shifting views of business, see Wyn Grant, 'Business Interests and the British Conservative Party', *Government and Opposition* 15:2, 1980; on the business attitude to Thatcher's destruction of manufacturing capital, see Dennis Kavanagh, *Thatcherism and British Politics: The End of the Consensus?*, Oxford University Press, Oxford, 1987, pp. 118–19; for a general overview of the Tories and Thatcherism, see Richard Seymour, 'The Tories: An Anatomy', *International Socialism*, 131, Summer 2011.

53. The City's dominance is antique, and it is materially linked to the state through a series of institutions from the Treasury to the Bank of England. Britain's financial elites have long enjoyed a special place in its power bloc. They organised informal British control of its protectorates in Latin America and the Caribbean, and coordinated flows of cash and commodities to and from the colonies. After the Second World War, they were less dominant, and their power waned as the colonial empire waned. The shift to a neoliberal policy thus represented a significant comeback for them.

been unbelievably high. Greece has stood perilously on the brink of collapse several times. And as Italy faced potential ruin, Angela Merkel and Nicolas Sarkozy both suggested that such a collapse would finish the euro. Jean-Claude Trichet, president of the European Central Bank until 2011, characterised the turmoil as 'the most difficult situation since the Second World War – perhaps even since the First World War'. The head of the Fitch ratings agency fears a 'cataclysmic' collapse of the euro. Sergio Marchionne, the boss of Fiat and Chrysler, has bluntly called 'the future of Europe' into question.[54]

The weakest link in the European chain is Greece. The pitiable situation of this country in recent years is hard to convey impassively. The impact of austerity is comparable in some respects to a major war: a catastrophic decline in GDP, such that a projected –3.8 per cent growth in 2013 was considered an improvement on expectations; a drastic and unprecedented fall in the live birth rate of almost 15 per cent; unemployment of more than 27 per cent; and working class Greeks forced to scavenge for food or queue at soup kitchens as a result of four years of sustained fiscal contraction.[55]

How to interpret this disaster? A certain contemptuous line of thinking says that the Greeks are being punished for being too lazy (although their working hours are among the longest in Europe),

---

54. Portions of this section are adapted from Richard Seymour, 'The European Meltdown', *Overland* 206, Autumn 2012; other key sources are Perry Anderson, *The New Old World*, Verso, London and New York, 2011; Guglielmo Carchedi, *For Another Europe: A Class Analysis of European Economic Integration*, Verso, London and New York, 2001; Christakis Georgiou, 'The Euro Crisis and the Future of European Integration', *International Socialism* 128, Autumn 2010; James Pettifer, *The Making of the Greek Crisis*, Penguin, London, 2012.

55. 'Gov't Data: Greek Unemployment Dips as Economy Claws Back Growth', *Deutsche Welle*, 19 September 2013; Helena Smith, 'Greece's Birthrate Falls as Austerity Measures Hit Healthcare', *The Guardian*, 18 September 2013; Heather Stewart, 'Oxfam Warns on European Poverty and Says "Greece is in a terrible state"', *The Guardian*, 12 September 2013; Helena Smith, 'Greece's Food Crisis: Families Face going Hungry During Summer Shutdown', *The Guardian*, 6 August 2013.

corrupt and venal.[56] The more sophisticated version of this story is the consensus among neoliberal policymakers and pundits that Greece is, if not already a 'failed state', then a 'failing' one. What does this mean?

There is a simple, if somewhat spare, definition of a failed state: it is one which cannot secure the means to reproduce itself, and is thus on the brink of collapse.[57] And there are a number of clear senses in which this could be true of Greece. At several points, the Greek state's internal cohesion has appeared to falter, saved at the last minute only by external intervention. Its political control over the populations it governs has clearly been pushed to extraordinary limits, and the dominance of the traditional parties has been seriously damaged. And its ability to deliver services is tested in the extreme.

But this is at best a descriptive category, which explains nothing in itself.[58] As it is generally used in connection with Greece, the concept of the 'failed state' is embedded in ideological assumptions that fill in the explanatory gaps. The narrative goes as follows: for years, this country's irresponsible and corrupt rulers offered citizens unaffordable perks, instead of reforming taxes; it allowed inefficient and uncompetitive practices to flourish in its state sector instead of disciplining labour markets; and above all, it borrowed beyond its means.

It is necessary to understand something of the nature of the European Union before this narrative can be unpacked. The EU is not a community of shared interests. It may be, as Perry Anderson called it, 'the last great world-historical achievement of the bourgeoisie', but the project of unification was always riven with antagonisms that would ultimately contribute to its ongoing crisis.

For its principal architect, Jean Monnet, European union was a means of rationalising Europe's outmoded polities and forms of

56. Alex Alexandreou, 'Exploding the Myth of the Feckless, Lazy Greeks', *New Statesman*, 18 May 2012.

57. This is usefully discussed by Takis S. Pappas, 'Greece's Failed State and Europe's Response', *Open Democracy*, 13 October 2011.

58. For a compelling critique of the concept of the 'failed state', see Charles T. Call, 'The Fallacy of the "Failed State"', *Third World Quarterly* 29:8, 2008.

production, while also easing the friction that had led to two world wars. Monnet, though inclined to seek equidistance between the US and the USSR, nevertheless sought and gained the support of US Cold War planners such as Dean Acheson, who saw in his ideas the basis for the economic regeneration of Western Europe under protective US hegemony, and unity against the Soviet Union.

The European Coal and Steel Community (ECSC), the precursor to the Common Market, initiated by the French foreign ministry in 1951 at the behest of Monnet, was a way of unifying French and West German capitalist interests with respect to the coal and steel region of the Ruhr. Stripped of supranationalist pieties, this was a French effort to prevent renewed German expansionism, to rationalise production in the economic sectors affected, containing the effects of intermittent gluts and shortages, and stabilising a state system under threat from labour and leftist insurgencies.[59]

In the new Franco-German axis, France would provide political leadership and Western Germany would serve as an economic powerhouse. This division of labour has been preserved more or less to the present day. The institutions developed by the ECSC, from the High Authority to the European Court of Justice, prefigured the institutional forms that would dominate the European Economic Community (EEC) and later the EU.

The initial model was not economic and monetary union, but a limited bloc of free trading nations. France used its political clout to block access for the UK, Ireland and Denmark to the EEC – partially on the grounds that admitting them would turn the common market into a vast free trade area subordinate to the US. It was the deep crisis of the 1970s that led European elites to fully embrace the idea of economic and monetary union. European economies had been left shoring up tumbling currencies, socialising private sector losses,

---

59. In the immediate aftermath of the war, communist parties in France and Italy were resurgent. Colonial insurrections were combined with domestic turmoil, particularly in France where a series of militant strikes broke out in 1947 and were crushed with austere brutality by the government. Unity among the core European states was thus partially a means of containing the influence of post-war socialism.

erecting protectionist barriers, and pumping money into national corporatist projects to regenerate growth. Meanwhile, following the collapse of Bretton Woods, the US was exploiting its position as the sole supplier of international reserve currency. It could allow the value of the dollar to drop, in order to boost exports, without experiencing the sort of currency collapse that would afflict European rivals adopting the same tactic. West Germany's response was to invest in new technology, suppress domestic demand in favour of export-led growth, and shift production overseas to exploit cheaper labour: a strategy that a reunified Germany has pursued to this day.

But the EEC's planners also tried to develop a common monetary strategy to restore stability in exchange rates. These efforts culminated in the European Monetary System, and later the Exchange Rate Mechanism. Logically, this entailed the deepening alignment of European economies, as no stable currency system could emerge while nation-states pursued radically different fiscal policies. Parties to the mechanism thus converged on policies of austerity similar to those already adopted in West Germany. France, which had initially sought to revive its economy on the basis of Keynesian nostrums, had adopted austerity measures by 1983. European unification thus reinforced the neoliberal turn. Profitability would be restored to industry through drastic cuts in wages and the unleashing of financial markets; currencies would be stabilised through reduced consumption (thereby easing inflationary pressures); public spending would be cut and labour organisations weakened; and demand would either be supplemented by overseas markets or stimulated by private borrowing.

Ongoing, low-key austerity policies (demanding low inflation, controlled wage growth, fiscal conservatism and flexible labour markets) became the bedrock of the Treaty of European Union (1992), and especially the Stability and Growth Pact (1997) that underpins the euro. An exceptionally powerful European Central Bank, informed in its inception by the ideology of German Ordoliberalism (a strand of neoliberalism), was created to help enforce these rules. Implicitly, each step in the integration of European economies demanded a further pooling of political sovereignty. Following the collapse of the Warsaw Pact and the absorption of a host of formerly

Stalinist states into the European community, the political thrust of integration became more important. Acceptance into the EU offered these states a means of rapid economic expansion after recent stagnation (while also supplying dominant European capital with cheap labour markets). But to qualify, they had to accept not only a plethora of economic and fiscal rules, but also the liberal political structure codified in the EU's laws and reinforced by its courts. With this centralisation and concentration of political authority in the EU, the logic was increasingly tending toward federalism.

All of this was enacted with barely a nod to electorates, barring some scattered plebiscites seeking popular mandates for decisions already taken. And, as the case of Ireland's two votes on the Lisbon Treaty shows, even an unwelcome referendum result can be reversed with sufficient pressure and blackmail. Organised labour occupied a subordinate role – for example, it was incorporated into the Consultative Committee of the ECSC – but otherwise, popular constituencies have simply been marginalised.

Underpinning all this is the regionalisation of the world economy which has reinforced the 'Europeanisation' of capital across the continent. The sociologist Michael Useem has described the development in advanced capitalist economies of an 'interlocking directorate': a network of directors sitting on the boards of multiple firms and developing a shared general perspective on the business scene. Across Europe, such a directorate has emerged over the last two decades to rival the similar networks connecting the US and UK.

This does not, however, mean that European union is a project of transnationalism; rather, it is the *internationalisation* of European states, their hierarchical arrangement under the hegemony of the US, that is visible here.[60] The ability of capital in dominant economies such as Germany to make profits in peripheral economies depends upon their being organised in a hierarchy of national states. This is a pivotal 'contradiction' in the project of European unity; any tendency toward centralisation hits against limits imposed by its organisation

---

60. For a useful critique of the 'transnationalisation' thesis, see Nicos Poulantzas, *Classes in Contemporary Capitalism*, Verso, London, 1978, pp. 42–69.

as a chain of national states. These limits are visible in the failures of the Union, such as its inability to develop a centralised political authority to rival the United States, or its floundering efforts to pioneer a Europe-wide defence initiative. The lack of political unity has also thus far retarded the development of a single, centralised stock exchange of a scale which would enable the EU to compete with rivals.

The second 'pivotal' contradiction, as mentioned before, is the class antagonism structuring the whole project. The development of mass resistance to the Lisbon Treaty, whose provisions were inspired by the European Round Table of Industrialists, illustrated that unification was not taking place in a way that incorporated all classes. Indeed, the success of wage repression across the EU, where the share of income going to labour has fallen on average by more than 10 per cent, is to a considerable degree the result of policies pursued under its rubric.

The sovereign debt crises following from the financial crash and subsequent recession have exposed the combination of class antagonism and the core–periphery relationship in a dramatic fashion. This can be seen in the way that Greece's debt crisis evolved. French and German capital have depended on the country consuming beyond its means. Public and private debt ensured that Greece could function as an export market for German products, without adding to wage pressure.[61] And because Germany could thus maintain a balance of payments surplus, it didn't have to support consumption domestically through high private borrowing or wage increases.

European leaders have sought to resolve the debt crisis by protecting the dominant banks. This emphasis on finance-driven growth makes a certain sense, because the recovery in profitability after the recession was largely driven by a crude transfer of wealth – with wage cuts and downsizing – and speculation. It is in this context that Greece has been awarded 'bailouts' to cover payments to financial institutions based largely outside its borders, while almost all the 'haircuts' applied to Greece's debt have affected Greek banks.

---

61. For a detailed account of this core–periphery relationship, see Costas Lapavitsas et al., *Crisis in the Eurozone*, Verso, London and New York, 2012.

But in return for these 'bailouts' – in return for meeting the demands of the lenders, in other words – the Greek government has been enjoined to sell public assets worth $71 billion at fire-sale prices: public industries, post offices and airports, infrastructure and acres of prime real estate. Public sector wages have been cut by 20 per cent and taxes have risen to levels simply unaffordable for most of the population.

Meanwhile, the power of the EU Presidency, the Secretary-General and the High Representative has been demonstrated with their insistence on access to Greek ministries in order to oversee the decisions made by elected politicians. Germany has argued that this monitoring should be conducted on a permanent basis.

Insulating parliamentary decision-making from the public has been of supreme importance. When the then Greek prime minister, George Papandreou, proffered a referendum on an extremely controversial 'bailout'/cuts package in November 2011, EU leaders were aghast. Papandreou's move was a feint, intended to coerce the conservative opposition into abandoning their opportunistic criticisms of the package, but to the EU this was playing with democratic fire. The referendum was, of course, abandoned within days and Papandreou's resignation followed soon after. He was replaced by an unelected 'technocratic' austerity administration.

Greece, however, was uniquely situated among European states. Its power bloc had been constructed on the basis of shipping and finance, and its political elites had always declined to tax the rich. The result is that when some form of social democracy was constructed under PASOK governments, it was funded by the taxes of workers on the one hand, and extensive borrowing on the other. At the same time, this power bloc oriented toward integration into the European Union, where deficits were taboo – part of the permanent austerity built into the regime. Some cuts and restructuring eliminated part of the debt built up, and Goldman Sachs wizardry did the rest. Unfortunately, the 'credit crunch' proved a merciless reality check.[62]

However, since the fall of the dictatorship in 1974, neither the Greek Left nor its organised labour movement had experienced a

---

62. See Richard Seymour, 'Syriza Rising', *In These Times*, 6 July 2012.

serious defeat on a par with those inflicted on British trade unions. The social struggles taking off in reaction to austerity reached near-insurgency levels, and were perceived by many Greeks – well before Papandreou's nadir – as a 'popular uprising'. In the years between the beginning of Papandreou's government and the May 2012 election, there were 17 general strikes. The mass of small-business owners turned against austerity. The traditional social democratic governing party, PASOK, began to suffer an epochal decline. Eventually a radical left party compromising former Eurocommunists and various Maoists and Trotskyist groups came within a whisker of being the first party in the Greek parliament, on an anti-austerity programme. But it is not the case that the only reaction to austerity was to the left. A section of the population feared and loathed the Left, and protesters, and strikers, and immigrants, as much as they detested austerity and the rule of European bankers. Since the semi-fascist Laos party had collaborated with the austerity government prior to the May elections, the neo-Nazi Golden Dawn was the major beneficiary on the far right, and in subsequent polls it has overtaken PASOK.

This brings us back to the question of how to judge claims that Greece is a 'failed state'. The effects of this crisis on the Greek state seem to be as follows:

1) A profound legitimation crisis, as the traditional political parties have lost their connection to their traditional base.[63]

2) Declining coherence of the political apparatuses, resulting in deadlocks in implementation of power bloc goals.

3) The declining capacity of state institutions to manage the population, due in part to fiscal contraction, strikes and social rebellion, with a consequent turning of the repressive apparatuses of the state to authoritarian solutions. (Half of Athens police reportedly voted for Golden Dawn in the May 2012 general elections, and police collusion with Golden Dawn was widely reported.[64])

---

63. Peter Bratsis, 'Legitimation Crisis and the Greek Explosion', *International Journal of Urban and Regional Research* 34:1, March 2010.

64. See, for example, Paul Mason, 'Alarm at Greek Police "Collusion" with

4) The further penetration of international capital into the state, as Greece's indebtedness has left it vulnerable to being restructured to suit external imperatives, while it has fallen to the 'troika' of the IMF, EU finance ministers, and the European Central Bank to both discipline Greece's austerity leaderships and defend them against their internal opponents. Indeed, the very toxicity of the Greek situation created the potential for financial debacles in other European states with banks exposed to Greek debts, thus propelling penetration. Such dominance is entirely compatible with the interests of Greece's power bloc, which is why the state was so available for the implementation of policies that seemed so destructive to the economy and even the authority of the state itself.

In total, this amounts to a 'crisis of authority' for the Greek state; but, crucially, not for the other member states of the EU. The punishment of Greece has been effected without seriously damaging the political control of other national states, while the institutions of the Union were only strengthened. Greece has a strong Left and a militant labour movement, but its subordinate status within the EU has enabled it to be effectively plundered thus far, with some human consequences that recall the impact of war or a profound natural disaster. In this respect, Greece is precisely the 'failed state' that Europe's rulers, and its own capitalist class, wants it to be.

Far-Right Golden Dawn', *BBC News online*, 17 October 2012. The later decision of another wing of the Greek state, its political executive, to go after the Golden Dawn after the murder of a left-wing rapper is indicative that once again the state should not be assumed to be too cohesive.

3

Ideology

The ruling ideology is then the ideology of the ruling class. But the ruling class does not maintain with the ruling ideology, which is its own ideology, an external and lucid relation of pure utility and cunning. When, during the eighteenth century, the 'rising class', the bourgeoisie, developed a humanist ideology of equality, freedom and reason, it gave its own demands the form of universality, since it hoped thereby to enroll at its side, by their education to this end, the very men it would liberate only for their exploitation … In reality, the bourgeoisie has to believe in its own myth before it can convince others, and not only so as to convince others, since what it lives in its ideology is the very relation between it and its real conditions of existence which allows it simultaneously to act on itself (provide itself with a legal and ethical consciousness, and the legal and ethical conditions of economic liberalism) and on others (those it exploits and is going to exploit in the future: the 'free labourers') so as to take up, occupy and maintain its historical role as a ruling class. Thus, in a very exact sense, the bourgeoisie lives in the ideology of freedom the relation between it and its conditions of existence: that is, its real relation (the law of a liberal capitalist economy) but invested in an imaginary relation (all men are free, including the free labourers). – *Louis Althusser*[1]

Every now and then, a study emerges which purports to show how utterly wrong and ignorant the public is about all essential matters. On the face of it, it's often difficult to argue with that conclusion. A fairly typical headline in July 2013 read: 'British Public Wrong About Nearly

---

1. Louis Althusser, 'Contradiction and Overdetermination', in *For Marx*, Allen Lane, London, 1969, p. 234.

Everything, Survey Shows'.[2] In this case, a study by the Royal Statistical Society had found that the knowledge on which people made up their minds about issues from welfare to crime was profoundly in error. This was obviously linked to the government's 'austerity' agenda, and its ability to implement drastic policy changes with an arresting lack of friction. A similar headline from January 2013 had read: 'Voters "Brainwashed by Tory Welfare Myths", Shows New Poll'.[3]

This is linked to the genre of polls which tends to find that most people don't know where Harry Potter was born, or think Winston Churchill was an insurance salesman. For what it's worth, I am in sympathy with the basic idea underlying these polls: the human race is vastly over-estimated. But you can't just *tell* them that. More importantly, simply compiling instances of general ignorance and denouncing them is at best useless, at worst reactionary. It also betrays a misunderstanding of why people hold the beliefs that they do.

Orwell, writing on anti-Semitism in post-war Britain, was simply pointing out the obvious when he said:

> antisemitism is an irrational thing. The Jews are accused of specific offences (for instance, bad behaviour in food queues) which the person speaking feels strongly about, but it is obvious that these accusations merely rationalise some deep-rooted prejudice. To attempt to counter them with facts and statistics is useless, and may sometimes be worse than useless ... people can remain antisemitic, or at least anti-Jewish, while being fully aware that their outlook is indefensible.[4]

---

2. Jonathan Paige, 'British Public Wrong About Nearly Everything, Survey Shows', *The Independent*, 9 July 2013.
3. Andrew Grice, 'Voters "Brainwashed by Tory Welfare Myths", Shows New Poll', *The Independent*, 4 January 2013.
4. George Orwell, 'Antisemitism in Britain', April 1945, available at www. orwell.ru. I cite Orwell, despite his own anti-Semitic inclinations, because I know full well the pointless reverence in which he is held in English culture. If Orwell told you to put your hand in the fire, would you do it? Yes, you would. You absolutely would.

This is the thing about ideology. Think about the worst, most ill-founded atrocity stories that one has heard about 'benefit scroungers', 'illegal immigrants', 'teenage mums' and 'nightmare neighbours' (you have to say all these words in your mind with a certain scandalised 'The Sun Says' voice). Taking Orwell's approach into account, one can only conclude that the belief in these stories is rationalising an existing, deep-rooted prejudice.

An anecdote, if I may. I was campaigning with antifascists in Barking before the 2010 general election. The BNP had a more than alarming chance of gaining their first MP in this constituency, which had previously been a solid Labour seat. One of the BNP's successful myths was that demographic change in the area resulted from a council-driven 'Africans for Essex' campaign, which supposedly gave cash incentives to black people to move in and thus consolidate the ruling Labour Party's electoral base. The scheme referred to here was a modest social housing fund, open to everyone. Thirty-nine people in total, of various backgrounds, availed themselves of it. It hardly made a dent on electoral arithmetic.

As we leafleted, we were interrupted by a man heckling us, asking 'are you from round here? Are you local?' As if. In further conversation, it turned out that he was vexed by the apparent advantage that 'Africans' had in gaining access to local services. 'What's your evidence for that?' I asked him, quite stupidly in retrospect. He looked at me as if I had just turned into a brightly coloured flamingo and offered him a beak job. He said: 'I've *seen* it!'

No amount of me being patronising could dissuade him of this conviction. And there is actually no reason to disbelieve him – he did 'see' it. But some things have to be believed to be seen. Take, for example, the 'Africans for Essex' myth. The standard argument is that the BNP 'exploited' a real problem with a lack of social housing, and misled people about its real causes. Certainly, the BNP worked to connotatively link the demographic change in the borough to the area's housing problems. And they were not the only ones doing so. The area's Labour MP, Margaret Hodge, persistently and cynically reinforced these claims,[5] ignoring the fact that her local council

---

5. 'Call for Migrant Housing Rethink', *BBC News online*, 21 May 2007; see also Elizabeth O'Hara, 'No Place Like Home?: Addressing the Issues of Housing

and her national government had systematically failed to engage in adequate house-building, instead turning the local council into a *de facto* estate agent for advertised properties. Nonetheless, people's readiness to believe in such racial conspiracy theories indicates that the underlying ideological presuppositions – connecting race and place, valorising the 'local', assuming a zero-sum competition for government resources[6] – were already well in place beforehand.

People are not simply deceived. We are all immersed in ideology, an imaginary relationship to lived experience, and what we 'see' is significantly determined by this. Concretely, it is unusual for this to consist of one coherent ideological worldview, but of many partial ideological perspectives and tendencies, imbibed from families, schools, media, workplaces, and so on. Ideology is characterised not by coherence but by disorder; not by stability but by turbulence.[7] Nor is ideology simply a cynical conspiracy. Those, like Rupert Murdoch, who play a significant role in purveying the dominant ideology, also inhabit it in an important way. A look at Murdoch's hair-raising Twitter account is enough to confirm this. And it is important to begin on the right foot here, because if ideology is treated as simply a highly effective deception or brainwashing perpetrated by the rich and powerful, the effect is demoralising. If it was deception, how could one possibly prevail against the mass media and the dominant parties? They would always win.

This is the problem that we have to solve. Somehow, the Right has successfully transformed a crisis of capitalism, triggered in this case by the activities of the richest, into a crisis of state overspending caused by the fiduciary incompetence and stupidity of the poorest. They did not convince everyone of every aspect of their narrative,

---

and Migration', Shelter, October 2008, available at www.england.shelter. org.uk.

6. For crucial insight into these ideological coordinates, see James Rhodes, '"It's Not Just Them, It's Whites as Well": Whiteness, Class and BNP Support', *Sociology* 45:1, February 2011, pp. 102–17.

7. For an argument about this 'dialectical' quality of ideology, see Goran Therborn, *The Ideology of Power and the Power of Ideology*, Verso, London, 1980, Chapter 1.

which is too incoherent to achieve total acquiescence. But it has been sufficient to weaken and disorganise opposition. What is needed is a realistic model of how this has been accomplished, what the weak points in the consensus are, and what resources there are for a coherent left-wing alternative.

In this chapter, I will start with three key assertions. First, ideology is *material*. Not mere vapour, it consists of material practices which are condensed in various concrete institutions. It can't be dismissed too easily as simple illusion. Second, ideology is *formative*. That is, far from being simply a 'reflection' of a deeper economic reality, it moulds the terrain on which political and economic struggles take place, situates the actors, and defines the terms within which they construe their interests. Third, ideology is at some level '*correct*'.[8] If this seems like an incautious formulation – how is anti-Semitic ideology 'correct'? how is homophobic ideology 'correct'? – let me immediately qualify it. Specific ideological utterances, particularly of the type mentioned, are often wildly *incorrect*. However, they are not merely 'false consciousness'. In some sense, they give expression to, and operate on, some real, lived experience, and are successful to the extent that they do so. These points may seem rather abstract at the moment, but their relevance will quickly become apparent.

Austerity in the UK I: The Ideology of Elites

There is one criticism of austerity politics that is both true and, simultaneously, flatly false: that it is *ideological*. This claim is ambiguous and needs to be unpacked.

The soft opposition to the British government's austerity package essentially holds that it is 'an ideological mission to shrink government',

---

8. Indeed, Terry Eagleton argues that most of our practical knowledge must be correct 'since otherwise our world would fall apart'. Thus, a certain 'practical solidarity is built into the structures of any shared language, however much that language may be traversed by the divisions of class, gender and race'. Terry Eagleton, *Ideology: An Introduction*, Verso, London and New York, 1991, p. 13. Obviously, all of this reading is profoundly influenced by Althusser, Gramsci and Stuart Hall.

as Labour leader Ed Miliband put it. The parliamentary opposition has an interest in putting it this way. Labour has committed itself to significant government-shrinkage, much of which will harm its own base while the Tories protect their own. In such circumstances, it distinguishes its cuts as merely necessary pragmatism, as opposed to the Tories' ambitious, ideologically driven demolition job. Yet Labour's cuts, though slower and a little less deep, would in any other circumstances be considered a scandal. During George Osborne's emergency budget in 2010, the chancellor was able to remark that he had inherited from Labour plans for cuts averaging 19 per cent across all departments. (Osborne had 'merely' increased the planned cuts to an average of 25 per cent across all departments). This was why canny Labour right-wingers had urged colleagues to calm down the anti-cuts talk, knowing that a Labour government would implement similar policies.

If it is true, as I have argued, that there is no socially neutral way of resolving the crisis, it is hard to see how any strategy devised for it could not be overlaid with certain social interests, goals and perspectives. It is difficult to see how it could not be ideological. But those dismissing austerity as ideological mean precisely that there is a purely technical, non-ideological means of crisis-resolution. In this sense, the criticism of austerity as ideological is obviously in bad faith. It simply says, 'their cuts are stupid, ours are going to be super clever'.

Even if this was in principle possible, in practice it seems incredibly implausible. Simply to think about what this would mean is to expose it as an absurdity. It is not just that the scientific-technical jargon of power, its expertise, is profoundly ideological, expressing in some form the lived experience and perspective of the classes that dominate these discussions. To have a non-ideological policy would mean that it entirely escaped any influence from the long-standing ideological assumptions embedded in all the dominant institutions where policy is deliberated, debated, framed, drafted and institu-tionalised – from the media to the major parties, from the Bank of England to the exchequer, from the top universities to the courts. This is what I meant when I said that ideology has a *material existence* in practices and institutions.

Even so, there is a narrow sense in which the claim that 'austerity is about ideology' makes sense. No one can be totally sure about the effects of austerity but, in the narrow sense according to which it is just a series of fast, deep spending cuts, there is ample reason to suspect that austerity by itself will not end the crisis in any sense that even banking and business elites would consider sustainable. Business executives, city economists and investors generally seemed to believe in the arguments for austerity in this sense. Growth, and above all profitability, matter to investors. And this strategy, as I will suggest, may not be viable. In this sense, the criticism is that austerity politics disposes of ideology in a way that is counterproductive to the long-term interests of capital.

However, before laughing about how stupid the elites are – really, *that's why they have all the money* – it is necessary to grasp the *rational core* of the austerity argument. As per my rule above, there is a sense in which it is correct, and its opponents would do well to appreciate its strengths. I want to illustrate this by describing the emergence and spread of the austerity narrative in the UK, first among elites.

The bank bailouts were initiated in earnest following the collapse of Lehman Brothers on 15th September 2008. In the US, it began with the Emergency Economic Stabilisation Act, enacted on 8th October 2008. On the basis of this, the Troubled Asset Relief Programme was created. In the UK, there were two significant bank rescue packages in 2008 and 2009, totalling at least £550 billion. This did not represent a sudden mass conversion to Keynesianism among the world's elites, but a panicked attempt to prevent a complete global meltdown. It is easy to forget in retrospect just how much panic there was about the coming disaster. As David McNally recounts:

'I am really scared,' U.S. Treasury Secretary Hank Paulson confided to his wife on September 14, 2008, as the Lehman Brothers investment bank disintegrated, sending shockwaves through global credit markets. The next day brought Lehman's collapse, followed a day later by that of AIG, the world's largest insurance company. Before the month was out Washington Mutual would melt down, registering the biggest bank failure in U.S. history. Then America's fourth-largest bank, Wachovia, went on life support. A wave of European bank collapses rapidly followed.

So panicked and bewildered were global elites that Alan Greenspan, former chairman of the U.S. Federal Reserve Bank, informed a Congressional committee the following month that he was in a state of 'shocked disbelief' over the failure of markets to self-regulate. Small wonder. By the fall of 2008 the global financial system was in full-fledged meltdown. Worldwide credit seized up as financial institutions refused to lend for fear that borrowers would not survive. Stock markets plummeted. Global trade collapsed. Banks toppled. As shaken commentators invoked memories of the 1930s, two U.S. investment bankers openly compared the situation with the Great Depression.

'Our economy stood at the brink,' Tim Geithner, current U.S. treasury secretary, testified about those weeks. 'The United States,' he continued, 'risked a complete collapse of our financial system.' Canada's finance minister, Jim Flaherty, echoed this view, stating that the world economy had hovered on the edge of 'catastrophe.'[9]

Within less than a year of the state taking on these debts, the story had entirely changed. The crisis was no longer one of markets and corporations, but a 'sovereign debt crisis'. Overspending, not overproduction, was the problem.

The British austerity agenda was first signalled at the time of the pre-budget report in November 2008, at which time the Labour government was engaged in stimulus spending. The Conservatives, still in opposition, had been spending several years 'detoxifying' themselves, attempting to shed their image as a ruthless party of competitive capitalism. As a result, they had committed themselves to a careful strategy of accepting existing government spending levels (about 40% of GDP), while questioning the priorities. However, the emergence of sizeable deficits, and the government's emphasis on temporary stimulus, gave the Tories a unique opportunity to say that

9. McNally, *Global Slump*, p. 13.

spending would have to fall dramatically.[10] At this point, they began to execute a careful, choreographed turn, qualifying each hawkish new announcement by blowing a kiss toward the poor.

In April 2009, at the Conservative Party conference, the Tory leader David Cameron announced an 'age of austerity'. He suggested: 'Over the next few years, we will have to take some incredibly tough decisions on taxation, spending and borrowing – things that really affect people's lives.'[11] Without being too specific, he tried to link the drive for 'significant savings' to a democratic desire for more transparent, honest government. This was at most a weak hint at what was to come but, given the Tories' determination to be seen to be a party of 'social conscience' willing to spend money on the 'frontline stars' of public service, it was all the opposition could risk at that point. The narrative had, however, been established: the problem was not chiefly the banks, and it certainly wasn't capitalism: it was government overspending.

Within a very short time, City economists were calling for fiscal retrenchment, and the austerity narrative was being laid in the press. A compelling example was Larry Elliott's article in *The Guardian*, announcing the 'dawning of the age of austerity'. I choose this example because Elliott is a left-wing Keynesian, and was thus hardly cheerleading for neoliberalism. He wrote:

> These are the facts of fiscal life. The City knows them. The chancellor knows them. George Osborne knows them. Public spending will be cut and taxes will rise. All that is at issue is when, for how long and by how much. Certainly, the scale of the retrenchment will dwarf that of the 1990s, when policy was tightened aggressively after sterling's exit from the European exchange rate mechanism.
>
> John Hawksworth, chief economist at PricewaterhouseCoopers, estimates that a tightening of 10% of gross domestic product (GDP) – about £150 billion at today's prices – will be needed over

---

10. Simon Lee and Matt Beech, *The Conservatives Under David Cameron: Built to Last?*, Palgrave Macmillan, London, 2009, pp. 13 and 22–3.

11. 'David Cameron Warns of "Age of Austerity"', *Guardian Unlimited*, 28 April 2009, available at www.guardian.co.uk.

the next decade to both rein in the deficit and compensate for the effects on the public finances of an ageing population ...

The problems with the public finances began during the years 2003 to 2007. The economy was growing at a robust rate but fiscal policy remained lax. The Treasury had far too rosy a view of the government's tax take, and ran up a sizeable structural budget deficit.

That meant that when the financial hurricane blew in, the public finances were in poor shape.[12]

What Elliott reported as brute fact was, I would maintain, inescapably an ideological proposition. But the power of it as ideology was the fact that it appeared perfectly natural and inevitable. As the political scientist Mark Blyth puts it, austerity is an 'intuitive, appealing' response to such a situation, 'and handily summed up in the phrase *you cannot cure debt with more debt*'.[13] This is linked to the old Thatcherite trope according to which the state is like a household, or a little corner shop, which must perforce keep its finances in order.

As the 2010 general election approached, the hints of future austerity became more regular, even if still subdued due to the obvious unpalatability of the idea. Importantly, it became increasingly clear that both of the dominant parties intended to implement far deeper cuts than Thatcher had accomplished. This is where the Liberal Democrats were able to benefit temporarily. While not disputing the necessity for 'tough choices' and 'difficult decisions' – the preferred euphemisms which stress the emotional anguish of those enacting spending cuts as above the real distress of those affected by them – they professed opposition to the deepest cuts. They promised to oppose an increase in VAT, although in retrospect their industry spokesperson Vince Cable admitted that this was done to 'score a point against the Conservatives ... that was in the election. We have now

---

12. Larry Elliott, 'The Dawning of the Age of Austerity: Ballooning Budget Deficit will Usher in a Prolonged Period of Belt-tightening Over the Next Decade', *The Guardian*, 24 August 2009.
13. Mark Blyth, *Austerity: The History of a Dangerous Idea*, Oxford University Press, Oxford, 2013, p. 7.

moved past the election.'[14] They also promised to oppose unpopular tuition fees. Unlike either of the major parties, they seemed blissfully unentangled in the financial elites that had brought the country to ruin. Indeed, Cable was seen as someone who had anticipated the problems with unrestrained financial power. And the Liberals were the least damaged by the parliamentary expenses scandal.[15]

In the election, partly due to the efficacy of stimulus spending, Labour's crash was slightly less than anticipated, and the Conservatives didn't get enough votes to obtain an outright majority of seats in parliament, with just 36 per cent of the vote. The Liberals were in a clear position to negotiate to form a coalition government. It became clear that the banks were worried by the absence of a clear mandate. Many preferred a Conservative-led government to implement austerity with maximum severity. Some investors made this clear to the press: the 'market is looking for a Conservative government'. 'A Labour-Lib Dem coalition would be an unmitigated disaster for the markets.'[16]

Worse than another exhausted Labour-led government, though, would be a weak, ramshackle minority government susceptible to sudden collapse, and new elections. The civil service, however, had prepared for the possibility of a hung parliament leading to a minority government, and acted to prevent it. Sir Gus O'Donnell, the Cabinet Secretary – then the most senior civil servant and head of the permanent apparatus which governs the country – explained that the civil service had role-played scenarios involving a hung parliament in order to ensure a stable government. They told the negotiating parties that if they didn't form a coalition, there was the risk of a Greek-style default and social breakdown. And they drafted 'guidance' for the

---

14. Kirsty Walker, 'Vince Cable Admits Previously Opposing VAT Rise to "Score Points"', *Daily Mail*, 28 June 2010.
15. In 2009 disclosures to *The Telegraph*, politicians were found to be massively abusing their expenses accounts to pay for their private luxuries.
16. 'General Election 2010: What a Hung Parliament Means for the Stock Market', *Telegraph*, 7 May 2010; Becky Barry, 'Nervous Markets Put Sterling on the Slide at Prospect of Lib-Lab Coalition', *Daily Mail*, 11 May 2010.

negotiating parties, newly codifying certain practices in the state, in order to make a coalition more likely than a minority government. This ensured that a government could be formed on the basis of an ad hoc agreement between two parties that had never been put to the electorate.[17]

Why did the state bureaucracy feel it was so important to control the outcome of an electoral process? The impeccably ideological answer they would give is that they acted 'in the national interest'. But what a senior civil servant thinks is in 'the national interest' is unlikely to be identical to what his driver or valet thinks is in 'the national interest'. Thankfully, O'Donnell explained his motives very bluntly: a minority government 'would not have had the strength in parliament to be able to pass the tough measures that would be needed to get us through this problem'.[18] This view was absolutely consistent with civil service orthodoxy – the unelected leaders of the British state, and this was particularly so of O'Donnell, are fully assimilated to the neoliberal orthodoxy that colonised that state during the 1980s.[19] So, for the civil service leadership, 'the national interest' meant a strong executive implementing austerity.

Once in office, the coalition government acted quickly and implemented an 'emergency budget'. The overall impact was to begin the process of deep cuts and redistribute wealth toward the rich,

17. Alex Stevenson, 'Civil Servants' Coalition "Manual" Under the Spotlight', *Politics.co.uk*, 14 October 2010.
18. Alex Stevenson, '"God" Denies Coalition Meddling', *Politics.co.uk*, 28 October 2010.
19. O'Donnell's own weight and influence within government, having been in Whitehall for the whole neoliberal period, was considerable enough to justify his acronym 'G.O.D.' It extended, by his own account, to 'triumphs' in privatising key industries, taking the setting of interest rates out of the hands of elected politicians, and the introduction of behavioural economics as a principle of statecraft. His position on public spending, expressed well before the government assumed the banks' debts, was that the competitive pressures of globalisation meant that the government had to keep taxes down and – that old saw of downsizing executives everywhere – 'do more

despite the government's professed interest in helping the poor.[20] For the business press and investors, this was exactly what was required. The government was perhaps overly sanguine about growth forecasts but, as an economist at BNP Paribas argued, 'The pace of fiscal consolidation is larger than we thought and is probably rapid enough to keep the ratings agencies happy ... on paper at least this is going in the right direction at the right pace.' Miles Templeman of the Institute of Directors argued that the budget was 'likely to improve the economic outlook by showing the public finances are finally being brought under control'.[21] *The Economist* expressed commonplace business wisdom when it breathed a sigh of relief that the pre-election taboo on cutting welfare 'beyond a few token items' was over.[22]

This cautiously optimistic consensus was not to last for long. But here we have a thumbnail sketch of how the ideology of austerity took root within the banks and corporations, the dominant parties, the state apparatus and the media – all in a mutually reinforcing and consistent fashion. In each case the ideology is embedded within a distinct scientific-technical discourse: that of the economist, the company manager, the state administrator, etc. But the basic premises are constant:

1) The crisis is first and foremost one of overspending, and demands 'fiscal consolidation'. No recovery is possible unless the country's finances are put in order.

---

with less'. Nick Robinson, 'Sir Humphrey Praises Politicians Shock', *BBC News online*, 14 July 2010; O'Donnell quoted in Gary Daniels and John McIlroy, *Trade Unions in a Neoliberal World*, Routledge, Abingdon, 2009, p. 70; Sir Gus O'Donnell, 'Ten Commandments of Good Policy Making: A Retrospective', British Politics and Policy at LSE, 1 May 2012, available at blogs.lse.ac.uk.

20. Chris Giles, 'Poor to be Hit Most by Service Cuts', *Financial Times*, 23 June 2010.

21. 'Instant Reaction to the Budget', *Financial Times*, 22 June 2010.

22. 'Britain's Emergency Budget: Ouch!', *The Economist*, 22 June 2010.

2) Cutting spending will bring down the structural deficit and improve credit ratings.
3) By demonstrating the fiscal probity of the central government, it will give businesses confidence in the future state of the economy and thus encourage them to begin investing in growth.

The rebuttals to this are by now quite familiar:

1) In most cases, the sovereign debts were accumulated mainly as a result of the banking crisis, not because of spending beforehand. They were a result of reduced tax receipts, and governments absorbing the costs of banking bust.
2) Those being asked to pay the debt through spending cuts are necessarily the poorest, the least responsible for incurring the debt, and also the least able to pay it.
3) States are not like households. They cannot cut their way to fiscal security, because spending cuts undermine growth. This is the famous Keynesian 'paradox of thrift'. If one person cuts back spending during an economic downturn, they improve their ability to cope by saving cash. If *everyone* 'saves' during an economic downturn, the reduction in aggregate demand will drive down growth, incomes and thus also aggregate savings.[23]

Not only are the rebuttals convincing in principle – they are winning in fact. By 2013, the UK's economic performance was hardly stellar, and any reduction of the structural deficit was entirely contrived. As John Lanchester writes:

> In June 2010, in his first budget, Osborne said the structural deficit was 4.8 per cent, and that with three years of reduced spending, the figure would be down to 1.9 per cent. So how's that going? Well, by the end of those three years, after £59 billion of tax rises and spending cuts, the figure is set to be 4.3 per cent. Even that number was achieved only thanks to a kitchen sink's worth of

---

23. Blyth, *Austerity: The History of a Dangerous Idea*, Chapter 1 provides an excellent 'primer' on these arguments.

special inputs, including a £3.5 billion windfall from auctioning off the 4G telecom spectrum, and some exuberant, almost rococo creative accounting to do with the transfer of Royal Mail pension liabilities, state ownership of the Bradford and Bingley building society, and interest credit from the Bank of England's quantitative easing scheme...

If you reverse the creative accounting and add the interest from the quantitative easing back where it used to be, as a Bank of England asset, it adds 0.6 per cent to the structural deficit. That takes it back up to 4.9 per cent – higher than it was when the coalition came to power.[24]

Far from austerity encouraging business to invest and generate a windfall of growth and good times, companies are sitting on a large quantity of cash – the proper collective noun is 'shitload'[25] – which they refuse to invest due to there being a dearth of good profit-making opportunities. From this vantage point, it looks as though austerity in the narrow sense of immediate fiscal retrenchment is a losing bet.

However, as I've said, it is far more to the point, and far more interesting, to understand the *rational core* of this ideology, because that is what makes it resonant.

In general, large deficits are unsustainable. When governments borrow, they borrow against future earnings, future social product. In periods of weak growth, there is less notional future product to draw against. If governments become more leveraged and growth fails to resume, bond traders can tend to lose confidence in their ability to repay the debt, and thus drive up the cost of further borrowing. Beyond a certain level, the interest payments begin to eat away at

---

24. John Lanchester, 'Let's Call it Failure', *London Review of Books*, 3 January 2013.

25. The conservative figure in 2013 was £318 billion. This was quite an embarrassment for a government wedded to the idea of a recovery led by the private sector, and it led to the humiliating spectacle of George Osborne and Nick Clegg begging businesses to expand, invest and fight the forces of stagnation. See Richard Seymour, 'Never Mind Tax Havens – The Real Hidden Billions are in Company Coffers', *The Guardian*, 13 May 2013.

future spending and thus growth. This doesn't mean that cutting spending solves the problem. The Keynesian critics are right about this. It just means that in a sense *all the options are bad*.

Further, there was an underlying problem brewing for capitalist democracies. New Labour had run up a significant deficit in the context of a precarious, finance-driven boom.[26] Many European economies maintained deficits at higher than 3 per cent of GDP in violation of the 'Maastricht rule'. This included Germany, the most zealous advocate of neoliberal stringency. As for the US government, the Bush administration had deficit-financed war crimes of staggering proportions before Wall Street's property bubble burst around it. The point here is not to condemn 'profligacy' in spending, but to identify a structural gap between the neoliberal commitment to balanced budgets and the cost of running a modern capitalist democracy. Since businesses were unwilling to tolerate high taxes, and politically powerful enough to resist them, governments could only raise revenue through growth, which wasn't tremendously high, or politically unpopular taxes on consumption. The alternative was to cut spending which, protecting core infrastructural investments and business subsidies, would mean cutting popular services and welfare provisions. Such are the competing pulls in a democratic class polity, and states found that running a deficit was the only feasible way to reconcile all of their commitments. Austerity in this sense can be seen as partially an attempt to shift the balance of class forces and thus change the definition of what is politically viable. And provided one shares the interests of businesses and state managers, or merely accepts their purview as the most valid, it makes perfect sense.

Finally, there is a paucity of plausible alternatives. Despite the brief revival of Keynes (and even risqué references to Marx in some quarters), the most prestigious technical expertise came from within a neoliberal purview, particularly that offered by neoclassical economists. Policy is almost always framed with reference to policy-relevant academic and think-tank research. When the British government implemented the first of its spending cuts, it explicitly

---

26. Not as significant as the deficit under John Major, and only after establishing a surplus through four years of a fiscal strait-jacket.

referenced research by the leading economists Kenneth Rogoff and Carmen Reinhart, suggesting that fiscal consolidation was the most effective means of restoring growth. These were not just extremely high-profile experts, they condensed in their biographies the perspectives and experiences of having worked in Bear Stearns, the Federal Reserve and the IMF. They were part of the elite, and part of the system they were trying to conserve. Of course, the British government could have chosen to listen to other expert opinion, from the likes of Paul Krugman, or former monetary policy committee member Danny Blanchflower, who argued for investment and stimulus. But they were marginal within their profession, and within the dominant institutions (including the monetary policy committee). And their recommendations did not gel with the interests of the dominant fractions of capital, above all the bankers.

It transpired that Rogoff and Reinhart's research was fatally undermined by some spreadsheet errors, which were exposed by an economics student.[27] It has been suggested that this could undermine the chancellor's austerity programme. But this is simply not to think through what is involved. The Treasury is stacked with eager experts, all more or less trained in the same neoclassical economic theory. It is part of a state dominated by a civil service elite that shares the broad precepts of this thinking. It is linked with a series of institutions, from academia to the City, which reinforce it. The Rogoff/Reinhart debacle does not significantly alter the *balance of ideological forces* within British elites. Short of a more severe crisis, a profound social disturbance, or a more concerted challenge from the political left and labour movement than has been seen since the poll tax, the most likely result is that the Treasury will prudently adapt its course in response to fluctuating events while remaining within the same broad paradigm.

The dominant ideology, the ideology of the ruling class, is not a malign conspiracy, but nor is it stupidity. The ruling class lives this ideology, because it resonates with its interests, its experience, and its accumulated expertise.

---

27. Charles Arthur and Phillip Inman, 'The Error that Could Subvert George Osborne's Austerity Programme', *The Guardian*, 18 April 2013.

Austerity in the UK II: The Ideology of 'Public Opinion'

Thus far I have focused on using the example of the UK to consider how and why austerity obtains the consent of elites. This is justified. The attitude of elites is not a matter of indifference for the Left. Finding ways to exploit their shortcomings, inconsistencies and divisions, is crucial. However, the consent of 'the general public' is a far greater problem. It is of considerable significance for this discussion that the 'emergency budget' welcomed by businesses and bankers was also broadly supported by the majority of the public. Moreover, with some important exceptions, significant elements of the austerity agenda gained a degree of popular support overall.[28] It is necessary to qualify this with two obvious points:

1) *It doesn't have to be popular.* In the era of 'There Is No Alternative', policies with little public support can be, and are, successfully implemented, often with little friction. Consider New Labour's wildly unpopular PFI schemes which, barring some very low-key trade union opposition and the odd localised campaign, were easily imposed. This is partially because the majority of those who would be in opposition have been excluded from effective political activity, and partially because governments are adept at directing subtle material incentives in order to help ease the passage of difficult measures. A refinement of the same point would be: it doesn't have to be supported by a majority. A significant and sufficient popular base can be composed of a minority of the public, provided others acquiesce. Thatcherism, for example, never won the support of the majority of voters. And indeed, the experience of Thatcherism in government drove opinions to the left. But for the majority of Thatcher's reign, she commanded a significant bulwark of popular support that was more cohesive and wielded more social power than did the opponents of Thatcherism.

2) *There is no such thing as public opinion.* The sociologist Pierre Bourdieu once wrote that public opinion is an 'artifact, pure and

---

28. See 'Yougov's Post Budget Poll', *UK Polling Report*, 24 June 2010.

simple, the function of which is to dissemble that the state of opinion at any given moment is a system of forces and tensions and that nothing is more inadequate for representing the state of opinion than a percentage'.[29] Polls can offer snapshots of a certain balance of opinions at a given moment, or they can detect long-term trends, but nothing in the sleek simplicity of the numbers should be interpreted as 'public opinion'. Polls cannot well reflect the fact that opinions are complex, ambivalent and layered, nor that large numbers of people simply don't know what to think, having not thought about an issue, or being too cautious to be definite. One of the reasons why people give 'thick' answers to polling questions is that they feel pressured in the interview situation to give a quick answer to something they haven't thought about recently. Polls also have trouble reflecting the fact that not all opinions are equal, or formed in the same way. Some are formed with little conviction or experience, some with a lot. Some are purely indicative of how effective an advertising campaign has been, others reflect life-long labour. Some opinions will shape individual and collective behaviour far more than others. And some people are better placed to act on their opinions than others. The term 'public opinion' tends to iron out these complexities.

With that said, if the polls can be taken as at least broadly indicative, what they show ought to give anyone on the Left pause. Certainly, there is questioning of the extent of the cuts and the fairness of their implementation. But quite often the cuts that are most popular are those which target the weakest – the recipients of unemployment, disability and housing benefits, for example. In the context of a crisis in which more people are dependent on the welfare state, popular support for it has weakened.

Underlying this is a long process of change in popular ideologies, which was partially registered in the 27th British Social Attitudes Survey (2009). It found that in 2009 public opinion was almost

---

29. Quoted in Normand Baillargeon, *A Short Course in Intellectual Self Defense*, Seven Stories Press, New York, 2007, pp. 145–6.

as right-wing as in 1979, and in its summary of findings stated: 'The public now appear less supportive of "big government" than at any time since the late 1970s.'[30] This is consistent with a series of polls indicating declining support for the welfare state and public spending.

The change since 1987, according to Ipsos-Mori's results, is staggering. Whereas in the late 1980s between 50 and 60 per cent of people supported raising welfare spending, even if it increased taxes, the figure in the late 2000s fell well below 30 per cent, with as many as 40 per cent opposed. This coincided with another change, as more people are likely to see themselves as being on a medium rather than low income. The change was particularly marked among young people. In general, the positive view of the welfare state, as 'one of Britain's proudest achievements' that predominates among older people is far less evident among the young. They are less likely to support the government bearing responsibility for the care of the elderly, and are among the most likely (apart from the pre-Second World War generation) to say that less generous benefits would force people 'to stand on their own two feet'.[31] If anything, the credit crunch and recession seemed to accelerate the reversal and drive people further to the right.

This was linked to another set of beliefs, also picked up by the British Social Attitudes Survey. While the majority of people were inclined to think the distribution of income unfair, and have *tacitly* redistributive attitudes, they increasingly entertained 'meritocratic' attitudes to success. That is, they more and more believed that hard work, ambition and a good education were the key to achievement. And they were much less inclined to think that other factors, such as race or economic background, were important. Meritocracy is, in general, a right-wing idea.[32] A modern form of social Darwinism, it nonetheless seems vaguely synonymous with 'fairness' and

---

30. *British Social Attitudes: 27th Report*, NatCen, December 2010, available at www.natcen.ac.uk.

31. See Ipsos Mori – Generations, available at www.ipsos-mori-generations. com.

32. See Seymour, *The Meaning of David Cameron*, Chapter 2.

'classlessness', and gained wider acceptance when championed by New Labour as such. The acceptance of meritocratic ideas doesn't automatically benefit the Right on every issue. The importance of education for meritocracy is one reason why soaring tuition fees were so unpopular. Likewise, extreme wealth inequality is also distrusted for those who believe success ought to derive from hard work, which means that there is a basis for some redistributive politics – the 50p higher income tax rate introduced by Gordon Brown's government was very popular. But it is easy to see how, in the context of a meritocratic ideology which places all the emphasis on individual effort, the plight of the weak and poor ('shiftless', 'feckless', 'layabouts') would generate less sympathy.

Writing in *The Guardian*, John Harris wrote movingly about this state of affairs, bemoaning particularly the self-defeating attitude of working class kids who blame themselves for a failure of the system:

I met a 27-year-old man who had just managed to re-enter the world of work, though the only thing he could find was a temporary contract delivering sofas. Around us were shelves peppered with self-help books; the people in charge assured me that even if work seemed thin on the ground, the people they supervised could always look for 'hidden jobs'. So I wondered: did he think that the fact he was unemployed was his fault?

His reply was just this side of heartbreaking. 'Yeah,' he said. 'I do. I think I should have applied for more. I should have picked myself up in the morning, got out, come to a place like this – tried more. When you're feeling down, you start blaming the world for your mistakes – you feel the world owes you. And it doesn't. You owe the world: you have to motivate yourself, and get out there, and try.'

There it was again: the up-by-the-bootstraps Conservatism of Norman Tebbit and Margaret Thatcher, largely unchallenged during the New Labour years, and now built into millions of young lives as a simple matter of fact. Oh, Generation Y. Why?[33]

---

33. John Harris, 'Generation Y: Why Young Voters are Backing the Conservatives', *The Guardian*, 26 June 2013.

In fairness, and as Harris acknowledged, this is far from the only discernible trend in opinion. Support for the NHS seemed to increase significantly among all age groups, and there were far more progressive views on sexuality and gender, as well as those issues known by the euphemism 'integration', among younger people.[34]

And nor has popular support for austerity been uncomplicated. While it is widely accepted that there is a need for significant cuts in spending, the scale and speed of these was contested early on.[35] Moreover, many of the measures included in George Osborne's first austerity budget were populist feints such as a small windfall tax on banks, designed to give the impression that the government was cracking down on the parasites and helping the poor, despite the overall impact of the budget. This sweetened the deal for many people who were resigned to the bitter pill of cutbacks. Other measures, such as increasing the rate of VAT, were unpopular. There is also a distinction to be made between those who reluctantly and without malice accept the need for austerity, those who accept it because they accept the scapegoating of 'scroungers', and those who avidly cheerlead it, agitate for it, and help demonise its victims. Nonetheless, the fact remains: overall, a government with weak democratic legitimacy managed to begin its term by introducing a programme of deep cuts that no one had voted for, and gained the support of a majority of people in doing so.

What explains the trend against welfarism?[36] Why are particularly younger people, including many of the people who actually need welfare the most, turning against it?

---

34. Indeed, the dovetailing of a certain kind of social liberalism with austerian ideology is probably not accidental: the neoliberal 'entrepreneurial' self has no inherent reason to defer to traditional values.

35. By September 2010, there was majority opposition to the depth and speed of Osborne's cuts. Bethany Clarke, 'Too Soon, Too Deep, Say Majority of Voters as Coalition Loses Cuts Debate', *The Times*, 13 September 2010.

36. There is an old saw that the public moves to the Right under Labour governments, and moves to the Left under Conservative governments. In this light, one could complacently wait for the experience of a vindictive Tory administration to drive people back to the Left – and the Circle of Life

Here, I think it would be useful to return to Gramsci's concept of hegemony. In the sense deployed here, hegemony refers to a particular mode of rule. In normal conditions, the ruling class of a society cannot simply rule by diktat. It must show moral and intellectual leadership. It must seem to rule, in a sense, for 'the whole' ('the national interest') rather than just its own particularist interests. Part of this involves exerting decisive strategy control over the main apparatuses in which ideology is produced – universities, church, media, think-tanks, parliament, and so on. But it also requires individuals, its 'organic intellectuals', who are able to explain, justify and offer direction to class domination. They must explain why the interests and perspectives of the dominant classes are *universal*. It must create a *common sense* – a set of ideas and dispositions that are gradually sedimented into everyday life and conversation, and which are taken for granted.

Yet, to stress again, people can't simply be manipulated into having opinions which have nothing to say to them. A dominant ideology, for it to be effective, must incorporate some of the interests and perspectives of the dominated. It must provide answers that resonate with their own ambitions and experiences. It must somehow assemble broad coalitions of people with quite distinct and sometimes antagonistic identities and interests. This is obviously a constant process of negotiation and construction. Hegemony is never a finished state, but always one that is being aimed at. Thus, a political project can be deemed hegemonic in aspiration if it attempts to produce a new common sense as the basis for a new type of political rule, and hegemonic in practice to the extent that it has at least partial success in doing so.

This is not to reduce hegemony to consent. As Nicos Poulantzas put it:

> Physical violence and consent do not exist side by side like two calculable homogeneous magnitudes, related in such a way that

---

will be complete. Alas, this comforting explanation is both mechanistic (that's a bad thing) and unable to explain the long-term, generational and complex nature of the changes taking place.

more consent corresponds to less violence. Violence-terror always occupies a determining place – and not merely because it remains in reserve, coming into the open only in critical situations. *State-monopolized physical violence permanently underlies the techniques of power and mechanisms of consent: it is inscribed in the web of disciplinary and ideological devices: and even when it is not directly exercised it shapes the materiality of the social body upon which domination is brought to bear.*[37]

This is quite a significant insight. There is a tendency on the Left to think that when the system turns violent, that is a sign of weakness, of the fragility of its forms of consent. It may sometimes be. In Chapter 2, however, I identified the central role of political violence in securing the neoliberal social order. And here we see that it isn't simply a matter of repressing the malcontents, banging up rioters, punishing the homeless and vagrant. It is about securing consent by changing the calculus of social behaviour. It is about *creating and policing the social categories through which consent is constructed in the first instance.*

Take an example. The British police, like no other police force, has embraced the tactic of kettling, in which police surround protesters and keep them confined in a small place only allowing them out in small numbers after a period of hours. It works in three ways. First, it is *managed violence*: it creates mobile frontiers where a confrontation with angry crowds can happen within a predictable range of circumstances, with police able to concentrate their forces at certain points when necessary and according to the geographical terrain already incorporated into the kettling plan. Second, it is *biopower*: it acts on the fact that people have biological needs and tendencies, that they need to excrete, that they become cold and tired, that they have caloric requirements which, unsatisfied, leave them physically

---

37. Poulantzas, *State, Power, Socialism*, p. 81. It seems that Poulantzas thought he was correcting a faulty conception in Gramsci, but in fact was far closer to Gramsci's intended meaning than many of his adherents. See Peter Thomas, 'Conjuncture of the Integral State?: Poulantzas's Reading of Gramsci', in Gallas et al., *Reading Poulantzas*.

weak and vulnerable. This is part of their deterrent against future participation in demonstrations. Third, it is *ideology*. The very act of 'kettling' people communicates to observers that they are dangerous criminals, if not bestiary. If something is illegal, or treated as such, this is automatically a reason for people to suspect it is wrong. It also creates the scenario, the conflict, through which this point can be 'proved'. Notwithstanding the problems it has had in the courts, this has been one of the most effective means of shutting down protest movements that are threatening to gain momentum.

In this tactic, coercion and consent, violence and ideology, are combined. The 'rule of law' is the dominant form of the dominant ideology, the main area in which consent is organised; and it is precisely through violence that it is materialised. Thus, it isn't that the state turns to violence when consent has been exhausted, but rather that it must reorganise and re-deploy violence in the constitution of social categories (race, culture, nationality, citizenship, criminality, subversion, entitlement, rights, etc.) to found consent on a new basis. It is therefore mistaken to see violence as 'making up for' a lack of consent, as a factor merely held 'in reserve' for when consent erodes.

What we are living through today is, in part, the fruits of a long-term attempt to transform the popular 'common sense' which initially went by the name of Thatcherism.[38] Thatcherism was a particularly British mediation of a neoliberal transformative project that had global reach and ambition. The transformations wrought cannot be reduced to neoliberalism, instead articulating many distinctive and heterogeneous elements drawn from embedded English traditions to its neoliberal core.

The ultimate success of Thatcherism in changing the popular 'common sense' cannot be reduced to ideology. In order to win, the Thatcherites had to exploit a grave crisis in the post-war institutions,

---

38. By far the best accounts of Thatcherism are: Hall et al., *Policing the Crisis: Mugging, the State and Law and Order*; Stuart Hall and Martin Jacques, eds., *The Politics of Thatcherism*, Lawrence & Wishart, London, 1983; Gamble, *The Free Economy and the Strong State*; and Bob Jessop, Kevin Bonnett, Simon Bromley and Tom Ling, *Thatcherism: A Tale of Two Nations*, Polity Press, Cambridge, 1988.

a crisis of governability, and propose a set of solutions that were amenable to the interests of capital. They had to politically defeat their opponents – not just the militant Left, and not just the Labour Party, but also the old Tory establishment and sectors of the state bureaucracy. They had to win influence and power in apparatuses from think-tanks and the popular press to business and parliament. They had to use political violence against strikers, rioters and protesters. And they had to deploy a set of material incentives, restructuring the calculus of loss and reward so as to make it harder to pursue collectivist solutions to social problems.

Nonetheless, it is worth briefly anatomising the specifically ideological and cultural moments in the Thatcherite project. It is often assumed that at its core is the assertion of moral individualism against collectivism, from which flows the language of Thatcherite 'liberty' and all of the chains of meaning that follow. However, I think Philip Mirowski is closer to the truth when he insists that the capitalist enterprise, not the bourgeois individual, is the model of behaviour that neoliberalism extols. When Mrs Thatcher said 'there is no such thing as society', only individuals and families, it was precisely the idea of the individual or the family as a unit of production, as an enterprise like a small corner shop, that she enjoined people to embrace. In this sense, the rationally self-interested, self-maximising individual is nothing more than a unit of capital. And the competitive struggle between enterprises is what alone guarantees that the good will thrive and the bad fall – monopolistic behaviour such as trade union action, and state intervention for the spurious purposes of defending an incalculable and obscure common good, only tend to pervert this evolutionary process and keep losers afloat.[39]

From this perspective, one can begin to understand other aspects of the Thatcherite diagnosis of the crisis of Britain in the 1970s, and the remedies they began to implement in the 1980s. For example, Mrs Thatcher took power amid a recession, with a superficially plausible explanation for it and a set of policies designed to overcome

---

39. On the neoliberal ideology of the self, very far from the individualism of traditional liberalism, see Mirowski, *Never Let a Serious Crisis Go To Waste*, Chapter 3.

it. Britain was uncompetitive and unproductive, she said. Strikes and militancy were chasing away investment, and overpricing labour. She offered the example of the car industry – demand for vehicles was not falling, but increasingly the demand was for imports rather than British-made products. It had failed because decades of corporatism had failed. The state's insistence on picking winners had produced a series of lame-duck projects. The unions had failed the workers, by encouraging them to strike, raising the price of their labour power, and by enforcing over-manning, making production inefficient and costly.

The simple solution was to let the discipline of the market do its work; let bad companies fail, and good companies thrive; let the industrious and innovative prosper. In saying this, Mrs Thatcher operated on existing 'common sense' values, above all the relationship between hard work and just deserts. She also exploited what she knew to be a reality in the trade union movement, which was that most strikes were losing their militant edge and solidarity actions were on the decline. Thus, it was easier to say convincingly that striking workers were merely harming other workers.

In this way, Mrs Thatcher acted on a crisis, both of capitalism and of the Left and labour movements, exploiting the opportunity to pose difficult questions. You want welfare? We all want that, but the money has to come from hard-working taxpayers at a time when finances are tight. You want public services? By all means, but they are badly run and overly costly because of union power, and this will undermine them in the long run – if we are to save them we need to make them more cost-efficient, and this means exposing them to the whip of the market as well. You want to save jobs? The state can only promote failure and drive up inflation. And so on.

As important as the discourse, however, were the techniques of neoliberal governmentality. By changing the balance of risks and rewards; making it more difficult to pursue collective solutions to social problems; defeating the Left and trade unions; offering material incentives to pursue entrepreneurial solutions (buy your home and treat it as an asset; borrow money to gamble on various prospects; dabble in shares); and changing the molecular experience of everyday life with the commodification of more areas of experience – by all these means the administration began the task of subtly altering how people evaluated the social choices before them. Over time, the competitive, entrepreneurial spirit entered popular culture, manifested for instance in property porn and a wide range of programming based on social sadism.

However, Mrs Thatcher herself could only ever win a minority to her view. Crucially, the greatest successes of Thatcherism in shaping popular ideology only became clear after Mrs Thatcher's time in office, and owe a great deal to New Labour's acquiescence. Had Mrs Thatcher not succeeded in defeating the sources of militancy in society, and in eroding the material bases for trade unionism, the emergence of New Labour would have been unlikely. And what New Labour represented was a form of politics known more generally on the continent as 'social liberalism'. In this mix, two strands are combined: a dominant neoliberal politics, and a subordinate social democracy. The latter is continually being assimilated to the former through a process Gramsci described as 'transformism' – the absorption of elements of popular-radical goals and ideologies into the strategy and language of the power bloc, the neutralisation of their oppositional content, and their rearticulation as part of a pro-capitalist politics.

What the Labour Party chooses to articulate is crucial, as it is the main author and defender of the welfare state, while its constituents are the major beneficiaries and supporters of welfare. In so far as the Labour Party adopts neoliberalism, it must seek to win support for these ideas by communicating them in a language acceptable to the working class. Thus, New Labour did not merely grudgingly accept the involvement of private capital in the public sector; it avidly sought to build capital, and market-like structures, and pricing for services, into the fabric of the public sector. It did not simply acquiesce in demonising welfare recipients. It started by cutting benefits for single mothers not to woo the Murdoch press, but as part of a consistent outlook that saw the benefit as one that fostered dependency. It was under a Labour government that state advertising campaigns escalated the ideological war against welfare recipients, highlighting fraud. It was New Labour that popularised the concept of the 'underclass' as a feral, anti-social lot that needed extra policing – curfews and ASBOs concretised this category and gave it a cutting edge. It was Tony Blair who won plaudits for his 'feminist' stance in trying to 'empower' women by coercing them to join the labour market.[40] It was a New Labour government that first embraced the idea of 'workfare' in the UK, on the assumption that, far from accessing their rights, claimants of welfare were becoming dependent on freebies that they should be forced to earn. All of this it did in a language linked to traditional Labour aspirations of growth, employment and expanded public services. The end result was that 'public opinion' shifted markedly to the right – including, most importantly, among supporters of the Labour Party itself.[41]

* * *

It is also important to remember the rule that ideology is in some sense 'correct': the sense that it expresses an imagined relationship to lived experience. And here, part of the sharp drop in support for the welfare state can be linked precisely to a feature of the landscape that many on the Left assumed would lead to radicalisation – namely the declining legitimacy of Britain's dominant institutions as such.

Cameron's 2008 attempt to link spending cuts to democratic reform and transparency has to be seen in light of the crisis of legitimacy of capitalist democracies long preceding the credit crunch. In the UK, the parliamentary system and elected politicians had never been held in such low regard. This was linked to declining electoral participation, the hollowing out of political contrasts between the

---

40. Mary Riddell, 'Why Asda Woman Matters to Tony Blair', *The Observer*, 4 March 2007.

41. Already this is evident in the findings of the 26th British Social Attitudes survey. Alison Park et al., *British Social Attitudes: The 26th Report*, SAGE Publications Ltd., 2010, Chapter 2. The findings included that only two in five people supported higher taxes to support spending on health and education, the lowest since 1984; half supported a freeze on taxes; likewise only two in five supported redistribution of wealth, and only one in five thought benefits were too low. Above all, it was Labour voters who moved most – Tory voters barely shifted at all in their attitudes.

major parties as they all adapted to neoliberalism, and of course the litany of falsehoods used to justify the invasion of Iraq.

In mid 2009, a long-brewing scandal hit the UK political class. Details of parliamentary expenses were sought through various channels and finally obtained by the *Telegraph* newspaper by means of a leak. The leaked documents showed flagrant misuse of public funds, and resulted in criminal charges against some MPs for false accounting. By the standards of the banking scandal, this was piddling. Nonetheless, the leak was more effective for hitting politicians from both of the biggest parties. It linked the political class as such to a general aura of corruption, and it suggested a degree of contempt for the general public on their part. It gave the impression that far from being a benign deliverer of services and protection, parliament was an increasingly authoritarian, distant and undemocratic haven for spivs. Who would want to pay taxes for that?

The point here is that there is no necessary link between a crisis of an existing way of doing things and an ideological turn to the left. Everything depends on how these raw materials are used, how they are organised, by which institutions and for what purposes.

There is also an element of real, everyday experience underlying the increasingly resentful attitude to welfare.[42] It is very clear that the welfare state is not a universalist institution, and has not been, at least in many of its provisions, for some time. Welfare is often not experienced as a right of citizenship but as something you have to struggle for. The clearest example is the benefits systems itself. Recipients of unemployment benefit know very well they are not the bearers of rights, but intruders who should be chased out of the Jobcentre Plus as rapidly as the bureaucratic machinery will allow: 'Why are you here, and how can we encourage you to fuck off as rapidly as possible?' This is conveyed to them in every way, from the interrogative 'appointments' to the demand for proof of seeking work, to the referrals to useless training sessions, and so on. Similar pressures have been applied to the recipients of Disability Living Allowance. Means-testing has eroded universality in other benefits,

---

42. The following analysis draws from Stuart Hall, 'Thatcherism – Rolling Back the Welfare State', *Thesis Eleven* 7, 1983 pp. 6–19.

with the presumably intended effect of deterring many claims. There is no need to say how and why the benefits system came to function as if it were a vast machine that would work perfectly well if it weren't for all the claimants – it is sufficient to note that it is not experienced as a right, but as an alm to be begged for, a petty resource to be struggled for, or lied for if need be.

However, it goes well beyond this. In every public service there have long been geographical and social maps of privilege and exclusion, frontlines of competitive struggle over resources. Take schools. Even before all the mania of league tables and 'naming and shaming' 'failing schools', there were these hierarchies and little informal ivy leagues – middle-class parents already knew how to adjust their future home-buying habits according to catchment area, to get a decent Church of England school for example. The so-called 'postcode lottery' in the NHS is much the same, particularly when it is governed by internal markets, a tendency which will only be sharpened and accentuated now that the effective dismantling of the NHS has begun. Local council provision has always been structured along class lines and segregated by race, tendencies accentuated by the centralised suppression of local budgets and the quango-isation of local administration in the neoliberal era. Moreover, with ever larger areas of provision rationed by pricing (rather than the traditional method of queuing), there is no question of 'rights' in those areas.

And it is in the texture of this experience, in the spaces long since evacuated by social democracy, subsequently to be occupied and reconfigured by neoliberal praxis, that the claims of the Right have achieved some resonance among people who are not in other respects right-wing. All right-wing axe-grinding to one side, there is a very real seam of experience of state provision as a competitive struggle for resources won from oppressive, intrusive and often serially incompetent and inhuman agencies.

Even in the best of the welfare state, there is little that has led people to expect anything other than a vicious competitive struggle for scarce resources and services in which most people lose, most of the time. This must of necessity generate tremendous social resentment: every little bit that anyone else gets is suspect; it has to be interrogated, the beneficiary's worthiness tested. If there's the slightest suspicion of a character flaw, never mind a lurid story on the scale of Mick Philpott burning his children to death,[43] then it is assumed that anything the recipient gets is a fraud. Eventually, there is a point at which some people who are not natural Tories start to ask whether the business of paying taxes into a costly, inefficient, oppressive system is even worth it, and whether it wouldn't just be more sensible to 'treat people as adults' (meaning, as rational consumers) and let them buy whatever healthcare, pension or 'safety net' provision they choose.

To summarise: 1) there is a crisis in the system, but what is being offered as a remedy is its deepening and radicalisation, and this is most popular where it activates a language of social resentment; 2) the catalyst for the acceptance of this language is the practical experiences of millions which, paradoxically, are in many respects the product of earlier waves of neoliberalism, as well as the traditional failings of state bureaucracies; and 3) if we are to defend the welfare state in this context, we cannot simply adopt a defensive strategy. To conserve it, the whole ensemble of institutions we call the 'welfare state' would have to be sweepingly reformed and updated, to make it genuinely universalist and responsive to contemporary needs. The language of reform and modernisation has been abused by those who want to reduce, privatise and marketise welfare, but there is certainly a case for reclaiming those terms.

Example 4: Why isn't Shanene Thorpe a 'Supermum'?

On 23 May 2012, *BBC Newsnight* carried a news item about a single mother in receipt of housing benefit. The woman's name was Shanene Thorpe. Her interviewer for the programme was Allegra Stratton, a former *Guardian* journalist. Shanene Thorpe worked for Tower Hamlets council, and received help with her rent because her

---

43. George Osborne used the fact that Philpott was unemployed to suggest that the state should not 'subsidise' such 'lifestyles'. This was subsequently taken up in a number of media stories and political commentaries. For some examples, see Mark Latham, 'Mick Philpott, George Osborne and the Bankers: Distraction, Division and Deceit', *LabourList*, 5 April 2013.

wages were too low to support it. The context of the discussion was the government's Welfare Reform Act 2012, which severely curtailed benefits in a number of ways, one of which was that recipients of housing benefit would lose a portion of their income for under-occupancy of their residence.

The news item plainly reinforced the narrative behind this policy, which is that the recipients of these benefits are absorbing the wealth of the productive members of society and should be forced to 'stand up on their own two feet'. Stratton's strategy in the interview was to calmly interrogate Thorpe, challenging her decision to live in her own digs despite her mother having a perfectly serviceable two-bedroom flat in which she could raise her child. Stratton implied that a choice to live independently of one's parents was unacceptable if it had to be supported by 'the taxpayer':

> 'You're on housing benefit, you get help from the state for your housing. Don't you think that you should possibly have lived at home until the point at which you could support your own house? … It doesn't sound to me like your mother's flat is a bad place, so it's a choice you're making, and it's a choice that comes with a price tag attached.'

Thorpe was clearly taken aback by the line of questioning, and the camera lingered on her discomfort under interrogation. Following the interview segment, Stratton addressed the camera, and said: 'The government is thinking of saying to young people: if you don't have work, don't leave home.' Thorpe had obviously been ambushed. As she explained:

> 'Colleagues who'd spoken to the people at Newsnight told me: Newsnight are on your side. They want you to put forward a good argument against the cuts to housing benefit … Immediately after filming I was upset: I felt as if I'd been mugged. I'd been led to believe I'd be defending young people from benefit cuts, not defending my family.'

It was later reported that Stratton had rejected a series of interview candidates when seeking interviewees via Tower Hamlets council, insisting: 'You must have got people living on benefits as a lifestyle choice!'[44]

The coverage of the affair focused on the way that viewers were misled. At no point in the interview were those watching allowed to know that Thorpe is actually in full-time, paid work, and that she only needed housing benefit due to the exorbitant cost of living and working in the capital. This is a natural thing to focus on. Yet, clearly, such an omission by itself could have been benign. It is the manner in which this lie is articulated with a moral ideology that has got people's backs up, and quite correctly. As Shanene Thorpe puts it: 'I did not expect to be personally scrutinised, have judgements made about my choices and asked why I didn't choose to get rid of my child.'[45]

Of course, Thorpe, being a normal person with a normal set of mixed reactions, wanted to defend herself in the very terms of the moral ideology that was being used against her. In the interview with Stratton, she tried to explain that she wasn't looking for a 'hand out'. Later she admitted: 'Claiming housing benefit was something I struggled to come to terms with, especially because I have worked since I was 16. I found it embarrassing.'[46] Her Twitter stream was both indignant and defensive, pointing out that she worked hard, and paid taxes, repeating that she didn't agree with 'hand outs', detailing how she struggled with the decision to ask for benefits. Thorpe evidently believed in the welfare state, but felt it important to distinguish herself from 'scroungers'.

This moral ideology revolves around the dichotomy of stigma, and respectability.[47] Thorpe was revolted, manifestly, because she had been stigmatised: she specifically mentioned the way the programme

---

44. Shanene Thorpe, 'I Felt Judged and Victimised by Newsnight', *The Guardian*, 31 May 2012; 'Newsnight Political Editor Exposed on Spinning Working Mum As Jobless', *Political Scrapbook*, 14 June 2012.

45. Shanene Thorpe, 'I Felt Judged and Victimised by Newsnight'.

46. Quoted in Robin de Peyer, 'Shanene Thorpe Left Angry After BBC "Apology"', *East London Advertiser*, 1 June 2012.

47. This discussion draws from Hall et al., *Policing The Crisis: Mugging, The State, and Law and Order*.

compounded the stigma attached to being a single mother. She was a respectable 'working mother', yet had been made to look like one of *them* – a scrounger, a social parasite. These people, after all, are ultimately to blame for the recession and the subsequent social crisis and the galactic destruction of wealth incurred: whether through their feckless borrowing, or their dependence on unsustainable tax-funded welfarism. (Moreover, do you see what they do with the money? The gold chains, the twenty-four packs, the violent sprees?) To be one of these people is to be the cause of all our misery, and to be identified as such is to incur real social costs. This, palpably, is the source of the horror.

This is not to blame Shanene Thorpe for being horrified. She did not create the stigma; she is one of its victims. For if paid work, a commodity whose stock increases as it becomes more scarce, is the ultimate guarantor of respectability in English culture – this is a truism – it is so to the extent that unemployment and poverty are associated with a social demonology, an image of criminal violence, uncultured hedonism, and savagery. So, embedded in respectability is an image of an ideal life, part of whose appeal is that it is clearly demarcated from the dissolute lives of those whom people now call, without embarrassment, 'the underclass'.

Since paid work guarantees the demarcation, Shanene Thorpe had every reason to expect that she would be treated as a respectable person by the BBC. She could not have anticipated that a considerable, long-term effort is shifting the boundaries of respectability in popular culture. The ideologically coded but otherwise far-from-subtle reason for this shift is an attempt to suppress the wage bill. The accent may fall on benefits, but these are merely a social wage. The costs of the reproduction of labour, however they are covered, are to be reduced through this expedient of forcing millions of young people and their parents to share cramped accommodation. Even having paid work isn't a guarantee of respectability, now, if soaring living costs mean that you still partially depend on the social wage.

But who produces this social image of the ideal life, to which workers aspire? For whom is one respectable? Obviously, the answer is, in part, the people who produce social images: the class of professionals, from media and academia, to the upper reaches of social work and the civil service, whose function it is to reflect on social problems, critically account for them, and prescribe some form of intervention.

Stratton's metropolitan, upper-middle-class manners did not seriously veil her attack – but they did make it seem almost natural that she should be treating her subject in an abusive, judgmental, moralising way. Stratton deployed the skills of her class, their ways of speaking to social inferiors, with persuasive authority. She invoked what 'we all know' with absolute assuredness. It is not merely that she was well-prepared and well-trained, while her subject was not. These were simply the attributes of her location in the class matrix – every bit as much as accent, comportment, education, sartorientation, and so on. And it was she who, in this transaction, dangled the carrot of respectability. In general, respectability is something that is conferred by social superiors. Or, as Stuart Hall et al. put it in *Policing the Crisis*: 'Respectability is the collective internalisation, by the lower orders, of an image of the "ideal life" held out for them by those who stand higher in the scheme of things; it disciplines society from end to end, rank by rank.'[48]

Finally, it is important to see this interview in its context: the conventions of news broadcasting, the professional ideologies of media producers, the institutional ensemble connecting BBC professionals to government, and the role that the interview footage plays in the encoding of the ideological product contained in the programme. It is well known that scenes of 'actuality' are there in part to conceal the produced nature of what the news is bringing us: the scenes from press briefings, war zones, conferences floors, etc., reinforce the spoken narrative of the newscaster, and attest that this is just 'what happened'. Also corroborating the narrative in a different way is the 'live debate': it shows that 'we don't take sides', but rather explore the issues raised by 'what happened' in a way that reflects no partisanship.[49]

---

48. See ibid., pp. 140–2.

49. This part of the analysis draws from Stuart Hall, 'Encoding/Decoding', and Ian Connell, 'Television News and the Social Contract', in Stuart Hall et al., *Culture, Media, Language: Working Papers in Cultural Studies, 1972–79*, Centre for Contemporary Cultural Studies, Birmingham, 1980.

So, this is the 'window-on-the-world' view of the media. In real life, the actual 'message' of the media passes through a complex series of apparatuses, each with its own logic and hierarchies, before it is received and implemented by the viewer. (I use the word 'implemented' very deliberately – it is intended to have an effect, to be put into practice, otherwise it would have no purpose.) And in this chain of apparatuses, the media is usually articulated with several others which supply it with a product – the administration, the courts, the MoD, think-tanks, etc. The extent of this articulation is such that, for example, it makes no sense to think of the BBC as merely reporting on government policy. Like all media outlets, it is part of policymaking, a factor in its formulation, a vector for its promulgation, a condition for its success. So, one can't begin to look at how Stratton and her employers came up with this idea without looking at how policymakers, civil servants and, at a longer range, other sites of power outside the state (businesses, lobbies, financial corporations, other news media, etc.), have already determined that this is a suitable and urgently relevant topic.

The interview material combined the functions of the actuality and the live debate. And it was necessary for the purposes of the programme that someone more or less like Shanene Thorpe should have been the interviewee-cum-scapegoat here. It bore witness to the substance of the encoded message. Thorpe's situation was not the story, it was the raw material on which the story worked to produce its real message. As she astutely put it: 'I didn't need to be in it: the story had been told anyway, of young people adopting a certain lifestyle, and being a drain on the state. They could have put a screenshot of my face up: my lifestyle was irrelevant.'[50]

This is a case where the metaphor of 'intersectionality' works very well. It is not just at the intersection between ideology and coercion (wherein the new social category of the bedroom scrounger will be concretised through threats and evictions). It is at the intersection of class and gender, the point where women still bear the greatest

---

50. Shanene Thorpe, 'I Felt Judged and Victimised by Newsnight'.

burden of reproducing social classes in the form of unwaged domestic labour and child-rearing.[51]

In the government's attempt to reorganise production and change the balance of class forces, it is attacking the social wage, the remuneration one receives for a contribution to reproducing society that is otherwise unwaged. In doing so, it falls back on traditional 'family values' ideology, the ideology of patriarchy. As David Cameron put it: 'Family is the most important thing in my life. And I think, family should be the most important thing in the country's life, because it's the best welfare state we ever had. The family is what looks after the children and cares for the elderly and all the rest of it.'[52] The changes to housing benefit, of which the 'bedroom tax' is only one, are justified in part by an attempt to force dispersed family back together, so that the young and old are not the responsibility of the state but of working adults. This ideology renders the work of reproducing society invisible – so that even if Shanene Thorpe, in addition to raising a child, works full-time for a living, she can be faulted for not choosing an austere life in a small flat with her mother.

However, family values were not the only gendered aspect of the government's case. It has consistently said that work should be made to pay, by which it means that benefits should be reduced so that working for any poverty employer is better than depending on the state. This is linked to the entrepreneurial conception of the self

---

51. On the question of social reproduction, see Silvia Federici, *Revolution at Point Zero: Housework, Reproduction, and Feminist Struggle*, PM Press, Oakwood CA, 2012.

52. 'David Cameron: My Wife "is Eclipsing Me"', *BBC News online*, 21 April 2010. Again, the Conservative Party was not working untilled ground here. The previous New Labour government had relentlessly deployed family values rhetoric in the context of reorganising the welfare state and re-deploying the police to deal with social problems allegedly caused by family breakdown, absent fathers and so on. Meanwhile, its incipient Blue Labour replacement has been banging the drum for 'Faith, Flag and Family', omitting only Blood and Soil. A useful guide to New Labour's family policy is Mary Daly, 'Shifts in Family Policy in the UK Under New Labour', *Journal of European Social Policy* 20:5, 2010, pp. 433–43.

discussed earlier. It is said that waged work is the ultimate solution to poverty, and that drawing a social wage leads to dependence. The entrepreneurial agent takes risks on the market, gambles on a few projects, takes the losses as a lesson and tries again. Losing on the market is perceived not as a structural reality – mass unemployment, racial discrimination, and so on – but simply an aspect of the risk one takes on by being involved. In this perspective, the worst thing that can happen is for the state to get involved in supporting the 'losers', as this distorts the selective mechanisms of the market and stifles the evolutionary progress of accumulating more and better 'stuff'. Instead, the state's role is to incentivise and nudge people to fully assume this entrepreneurial perspective, to judge themselves in relation to 'the market', to embrace the thrill of 'risk'. Single mothers: don't just stay at home looking after children! Out-source childcare to an affordable babysitter, and take on multiple jobs and many personas.

Amid all this is lodged an anti-feminist wisdom that is sometimes packaged as feminism. In the neoliberal purview, sexism is not a structure of oppression but an atavistic male attitude. The 'career woman' can thus be seen as a feminist hero not for attacking patriarchy but for assuming the risks of enterprise and succeeding. Better still if she uncomplainingly assumes the main demanding roles of mother, social entertainer, charity fund-raiser, and perhaps even a certain kind of activism – many projects, many selves. Obviously, this is entirely compatible with traditional gender roles. Not for nothing, neoliberalism extols what the British press calls 'super-mums' – mothers with demanding careers.

Shanene Thorpe didn't qualify for this treatment, not because she worked less hard or was less worthy, but because she was a single mother, and because she was too far down in the class hierarchy.

Coda: Austerity Nostalgia and the Spirit of 1945[53]

I end this chapter with a brief suggestion about what *not* to do. In the 1980s, certain right-ward moving socialists such as Stuart Hall

---

53. This doesn't necessarily refer to the Ken Loach film. Okay, it does a bit.

tried to warn against certain backward tendencies on the Left.[54] They argued that the idiom of the Left was stuck in the past and was increasingly irrelevant to the realities of modern social life.

The strongest part of this argument was that the era of a Keynesian, corporatist settlement was over. It is not just, they said, that this system resulted in stagflation and social breakdown in the 1970s. It is not just that the productive base of the economy can no longer support the class compromise embedded in the Keynesian settlement. It is that people don't believe in it any more. The idea that social justice can be delivered by a concord between the top floor of the CBI, and of the TUC, and of the BBC, and of the government, is over. The *consensus* is over. It doesn't resonate with popular experiences.

In this context, it was argued, the Left had to take the leap and found its project for transformation on the bad new things, not the good old things. I don't want to linger on specific political solutions recommended by these socialists, largely because they weren't very good.[55] However, I do want to latch onto what was rational in their argument. In today's context, to evoke the post-war settlement strikes me as at best a defensive gesture which can only take us so far, at worst an unproductively backward tendency.

There is no possibility of returning to a post-war 'golden age', and it would be undesirable in any case. If you doubt this, I want you to phone the Forties and find out for yourself. 'Hello? Hey, 1945, we'd really like to borrow your bombed out craters, your rationing, your rickets and TB, your ripping music hall culture, your outdoor toilets, your entrenched colonial racism, your male breadwinner patriarchy, and your decrepit sense of deference. Because our era apparently doesn't suck enough.'

The Forties were *fucking grim*. No one, but no one, wants them back. I'll take the twenty-first century and internet boosterism every time. I am not saying that we should be casual with the remaining legacy of 1945, above all the National Health Service. I am certainly not saying that we should forget about defending welfare. I am saying that

---

54. See, for example, Stuart Hall, 'The Great Moving Right Show', in Hall and Jacques, eds., *The Politics of Thatcherism*.

55. Cough New Labour cough.

these objectives have to be articulated with a much more ambitious agenda, and linked to something more contemporary than an attempt to rehabilitate the post-war dream. The complex popular energies behind the Occupy movement, say, or the feminist insurgency.

For what is actually involved in any attempt to summon the spirit of 1945 is an attempt to somehow defend the welfare state and social democracy by recreating an era whose chief characteristic is terrifying want, squalor, crushing injustice, and early death. The implied belief is that somehow the experience of our own once-in-a-generation crisis, our own privation, can, through the appropriate political intervention, have the same unifying, galvanising effect. But even if this was in principle a good idea, the conditions that enabled the post-war welfare state have gone, and will not return.

The tendency to succumb to what Owen Hatherley presciently called 'austerity nostalgia',[56] abundantly apparent in the leftist squeals of delight over Danny Boyle's Olympics spectacle, has to be one of the most dispiriting signs of degeneration and decadence on the Left. It is the symptom of an exhausted Left, unable to relate to the cultural and political sources of radicalism today, whether it is the *indignado* movement, the feminist insurgency, student rebellion or flash-mobbing tax protesters. We need more Occupy Wall Street than Occupy Dresden.

In the concluding chapter, I will try to say what a more vital, modern Left might offer instead of a yearning look into the past.

---

56. Owen Hatherley, 'Austerity Nostaglia', *Sit Down Man, You're a Bloody Tragedy*, 5 February 2009, available at http://nastybrutalistandshort. blogspot.co.uk; Owen Hatherley, 'Lash Out and Cover Up: Austerity Nostalgia and Ironic Authoritarianism in Recession Britain', *Radical Philosophy* 157, September/October 2009.

Conclusion: Strategy

It is one thing to say that capitalist development is inherently rent by its own contradictions: That remains the great insight of Marxism. But what is wrong about fatalistic expectations of breakdown is not just that capitalism has consistently outlived them, but that they ignore the fact that the bourgeoisie is distinctive among ruling classes historically precisely because it cannot exist without 'constantly revolutionizing'. – *Leo Panitch*[1]

There is a tendency, when powerless, to console oneself with grandiose notions. The persistence of consolatory ideologies on the Left is thus no accident, but reflects both its weakness and its failure to adapt to its weakness. What are some of these ideas? Austerity is detested by the masses; you can't *do that* to people without there being a reaction. 'They' may be nasty, but 'they' are also weak. 'Their' crisis cannot be resolved (the less said about ours, the better) without a catastrophe so severe (world war, for example) that it will bring the masses into open political contest. The 'contradictions' of the system are ever-sharpening, drawing ever closer to an epochal showdown. Oh, and remember this one? 'Neoliberalism is dead.' Ha ha ha ha ha ha ha!

In fairness, such unworldly optimism has a certain valid basis. It's true that there is hardly an enthusiastic consensus behind austerity, and millions do hate it; that a crisis of capitalism depletes the resources of its rulers, and of the state, to rule; that the system is always unstable, always afflicted by permanent crisis tendencies. There is no guarantee of ongoing ruling class hegemony – this is something that has to be assiduously constructed and re-negotiated. Furthermore, any good left-wing activist knows the flashpoints of struggle well, and is immersed constantly in evaluating, weighing up

---

1. Leo Panitch, *Renewing Socialism: Democracy, Strategy, and Imagination*, Westview Press, Boulder CO, 2001, p. 16.

the possibilities for intervening and shaping them; the better left-wing activists know them so well that they have no time to idly reflect on how *bad* things really are. Hyperactivism has its consolations too. A half-decent activist also has a repertoire of informative historical examples to ward off nagging doubts: before 1968, there was a 1967; before 1936, 1933; before 1917, 1914. This essentially boils down to: 'it's always darkest before the dawn'.

If this book has been intended to do anything, it has been to find a way to drop those fetishes, as well as certain other ideas which impede us, assimilate the reality of our present situation, and soberly assess the challenge posed by austerity, without losing sight of the objective – which is to navigate our way out of this impasse. This is not a counsel of despair. I do not think it likely that the Left will be able to simply stop austerity in its tracks, and immediately reverse its successes thus far. However, it is eminently feasible to stop the worst of it, and in doing so to build up the forms of organisation, the political nous, the ideological strategies and the theoretical resources to start turning the tide over a longer duration.

I will have more to say on this later, but a crucial point here is that the Left has to stop thinking in terms of 'the next thing': a defensive battle here, a new front of struggle there, always hoping that it will be the spark that kindles the fire. We have to think long term in the same way that the ruling class does. If neoliberalism has been and is a 'constructivist' project,[2] one which actively seeks to create the types of behaviour and norms that it extols – one which, to parody a certain manner of speaking, seeks to *enter our souls* – then it seems to me that what is obviously needed is a process of socialist reconstruction. The Left's efforts need to be geared toward reconstituting at the micro-level the forms of social organisation, mutual solidarity and collectivism that can be resilient against the tidal wave of neoliberal experience.

It is no paradox to add that even if we can't stop austerity *in toto*, we should aim to do precisely that. And this is where even the most

2. This is the case made by Wendy Brown, 'Neo-Liberalism and the End of Liberal Democracy', *Project Muse: Theory and Event* 7:1, 2003.

pig-head 'revolutionary optimism' is preferable to the wretched fatalism of social democracy. Consider the rationale for centre-left complicity with austerity. 'We cannot', says the Labour leadership, 'oppose every cut.' This is said with the clear implication that to oppose all cuts is an unreasonably unyielding stance. Such was the line advanced by the party's Blairite right-wing during the brief period in which Labour was prepared to articulate a moderately anti-cuts, stimulus-based critique of the coalition government. The Blairite flack and gossip merchant Dan Hodges – once known as the 'Carole Caplin' of the David Miliband leadership campaign – sarcastically complained: 'What are we doing? Giving the impression we want to die in the ditch for every last Sea Harrier, millionaire's child benefit payment and pint of student snakebite.' The correct approach, Hodges averred, was to 'Match their overall spending totals, and hit them over priorities within that framework. At the same time ensure there are no uncosted spending commitments.'[3]

The obvious answer to such evasive manoeuvres is that there should be no cuts in *total* spending. There may be a case for spending more efficiently – but then, shouldn't they have been doing that already? Worse than evasive, Hodges' remarks studiously trivialised what was really happening. The Tory spending review that he was responding to had cut a fifth off public spending, and the Prime Minister had made it clear that he intended those cuts to be permanent rather than temporary. Students were not merely losing their snakebite: fees were to be tripled, and the Education Maintenance Allowance cut. Far from millionaires being the major losers of welfare cuts, cuts to housing benefits risked putting 40,000 people on the streets. And Hodges was not alone in arguing that Labour should accept this. Former party chairman Peter Watt, another Blairite, has urged the same stance, claiming that the party's mild opposition to cuts was hurting Labour's electoral chances. In fact, polls suggested that precisely the opposite was true: a significant number of people wanted at least some opposition to the cuts, which were seen as being

---

3. 'The CSR was a Political Disaster for Labour, says Dan Hodges', *Labour Uncut*, 22 October 2010.

too hard, too fast.[4] Subsequently, of course, the Blairites seemed to win this argument within the Labour leadership, which has not only accepted the logic of cuts almost in its entirety, but has particularly embraced the most socially sadistic elements such as the attack on welfare recipients.[5]

Leaving aside outright capitulation, a great deal hangs on whether one undertakes an offensive or a defensive strategy. From the perspective of a purely defensive strategy, there will be a tendency to accept some cuts to public spending as a minimal realistic concession to the opposition. This is inevitably the position of the trade union leaderships. Whether the bargaining table is in London or Wisconsin, the institutions of the extant labour movement are proving incapable, by themselves, of leading a broad alliance against austerity because of their narrow, defensive strategy.

In what follows, I will outline some elements of an offensive strategy – in fact, what logically amounts to an anticapitalist strategy. This is not because I have any illusions about overthrowing global capitalism in the next few years. We in the UK will be fortunate to get rid of Cameron in the next few years. It is rather because, in order to be effective even in securing the limited goals of containing austerity, winning some reversals, protecting core public infrastructures, making some democratic gains, we have to be prepared to build the sorts of organisations that are prepared to challenge and disrupt capitalism. Only this can shift the balance of forces significantly in our favour.

Ideology

How should the Left respond to the successes of the Right in shaping the popular understanding of the present crisis? It seems to me that

---

4. Peter Watt, 'Let's Learn From the Tories and Detoxify our Brand', *Labour Uncut*, 21 February 2011; Peter Watt, 'Labour Must Stop Fighting the Cuts', *Labour Uncut*, 19 May 2011; Lee Brown, 'Polls Indicate Opposing Cuts Boosts Labour', *LabourList*, 20 May 2011.
5. See Richard Seymour, 'Authoritarianism and Free-market Orthodoxy in Liam Byrne's Welfare ideas', *The Guardian*, 4 January 2012.

the worst response is to dismiss this question as insignificant, stressing the all-saving properties of 'the struggle' and 'real experience'. In its way, this is little better than the despairing cries of 4chan geeks and Anonymous types about 'the docile, brainwashed herd'. Both are simply ways of vacating the terrain on which ideology is fought.

There is no experience, no struggle, which is not lived through ideology. Ideology moulds the terrain on which social action takes place, and situates the actors. What Gramsci termed the 'war of position', the slow-burning ideological, parliamentary and cultural contests that are the necessary basis for consent and dissent, prepares the preconditions for sudden crises, sudden shifts in favour of one side or other, sudden eruptions of open conflict. The Right knows this very well, and puts the principle to work.

So with the importance of ideology and political subjectivities foregrounded, it remains to say something about how it is possible to effectively intervene. It is in the nature of ideology that it is never seamlessly coherent; it contains ambiguities and downright contradictions. Heterogeneous elements are articulated in uneven formations. The same person who favours individualism and punitive austerity in the case of the unemployed will be strikingly collectivist in the matter of healthcare or pensions.

Ernesto Laclau offered one of the most interesting accounts of how this works, with his 'theory of articulation'. In this view, ideological elements (concepts, ideas, sentiments) are linked together in ways that are often not strictly logical. Rather, they are bound together by connotation; by links that custom or repetition has established between them. Advertising works very much on this principle, seeking to establish connotative links between things that have no logical connection – between a luxury car and manly heroism, between a chocolate bar and an orgasm, or between fast food and happy families. The result is not necessarily a coherent set of ideas, but rather an unstable system of concepts articulated with one another. And when we are speaking of ideologies, there tends to be an 'articulating principle', a key element which 'quilts' or binds together all of the otherwise autonomous elements. For a certain type of conservatism, this articulating principle is 'the nation', for another type it is 'the market'; for most socialists, it is 'class'; for liberals, it might be 'the individual' or 'humanity'. This articulating principle can bind together profoundly different ideological elements.[6]

This can help account for that peculiar phenomenon in opinion polling wherein the same question, asked a variety of slightly different ways, with slightly different emphases, will generate widely different responses. And here, the Right has long understood something that the Left will do well to remember. Whatever the plane of crisis, whatever the axis of struggle, *the issue can always be put another way.* The crisis of capitalism became a crisis of overspending, just as the crisis of poverty became a crisis of social dysfunction. Here it is not a question of simply inventing a new narrative: to re-articulate issues in this way, the Right must operate on genuinely popular ideas (distrust of the state, contempt for politicians, paranoia and resentment of others); it must absorb certain elements of popular discontent into its own right-wing articulation.

To take one example, the policy of 'free schools' in the UK involves turning state-funded schools over to non-profit charitable trusts, independent of the local authority. The trusts could then be run by parents, charities, churches or businesses. (In Sweden, an example cited by the government, most 'free schools' are run by businesses.) Those running the schools can create their own curriculum, albeit within certain constraints and subject to inspection. The Conservatives, pushing the policy, suggested that this would introduce a competitive element into the education system, between private 'free schools' and state schools, thus improving standards.

Despite widespread professional opposition, the policy has been quite popular, with some 79 per cent of people approving.[7] It is fairly obvious why. The existing system is horribly inadequate. Local authority schools are often grim and underfunded. The curriculum and testing system in state schools is soul destroying. And, of course, in a society where competition is the cardinal virtue, anything that promises improved 'standards' for one's progeny is to be leaped at. Ironically, this is linked to the same 'meritocratic' ideology that led

---

6. Ernesto Laclau, *Politics and Ideology in Marxist Theory*, Verso, London & New York, 2011.

7. George Eaton, 'Education Poll: Yes to Free Schools, no to £9,000 fees', *New Statesman*, 25 May 2011.

people to be outraged by £9,000 university tuition fees. After all, if the basis of being able to participate in competition is education, if that is the font of all opportunity, then barriers to it are scandalous. This illustrates a) how real popular discontent, having *no necessary political valence*, can be articulated to a right-wing agenda, and b) how the same set of articulations can favour both competitive individualism and certain basic forms of collectivism.

In response to the Right's efficacy thus far, a good starting point is thus to look for the fractures and weaknesses in the dominant ideology, to try to extract the elements of genuine popular discontent they are working on and absorb them into our own perspective. For example, the implementation of 'means testing' in welfare, despite its practical effects mainly being felt among the working class, is often justified by accessing *resentment against the rich*: why should they get something from the state when they're already doing so well for themselves? This resentment is the legitimate kernel of a certain form of austerian ideology: people want to *punish* someone for all the shit that has been inflicted on them. And it is by no means beyond the wit of the Left to intervene in this argument, pointing out that such resentment is far better satisfied by the imposition of seriously punitive taxes. Jack up top rate income taxes to 90 per cent, then sit back and wait for some wealthy lower lips to start wobbling on television. Few would be stony-hearted enough not to laugh at that. This is linked to the necessarily fragile and provisional nature of the social coalition assembled by the austerians, which pulls together diverse and basically antagonistic class elements with diverse sub-ject-positions. It should not be assumed that present success in constructing such an alliance is any surety against future failure.

It isn't good enough, in doing this, for the Left to defend the status quo (or to defend it minus a few 'realistic' concessions). The logic, all too often, is that we must defend our previous gains first, and only then in the context of mustering the forces necessary for such a defensive fight will it be possible to tip the balance into something like an offensive struggle. This will lose, because the status quo is unpopular – not every aspect of it, but much of it. It is not just the banks that people distrust; in the core capitalist societies, people have never been more alienated from the dominant parties, the parliamentary system, and core aspects of the welfare state. The only effective defence, from the point of view of ideology, is an offensive that touches on these forms of dissatisfaction, and which exploits the ambiguities and polysemy built in to the dominant ideology. For example, they want free schools, with their own curricula, locally run? Fine, we want *all* schools to be 'free': free of league tables and constant testing and Ofsted inspections, free of bureaucratic targets, free from selection, free from enforced scarcity and irrational competition, and run democratically (rather than by businesses or churches). If the status quo is untenable, we must show that we understand better than anyone why that is, and have a preferable solution.

Nor is it adequate to stick to those issues on which the Left is strongest. For example, public healthcare is as universally popular as free education, while privatisations are generally as unpopular as ministerial snouts in the trough. On that basis, we could just tactically downplay issues like 'workfare' or immigration, where it seems the Right has the constant advantage of being better placed to mobilise social resentment, and stick to apple pie issues. Free schools and hospitals! Who could disagree? The problem with this is that it is opportunistic in the classic sense: for the purposes of short-term benefit, it makes serious concessions that will be more costly in the long term. For we will find that the same social resentment and grievances that can be turned against welfare can also be used to begin prising apart the consensus on health and education. It takes no great leap of imagination to see how: we can't afford to pay for these greedy unionised teachers any more, they need the discipline of the market; we have to stop subsidising these health tourists, a free system is a soft touch for spongers; why should smokers and the morbidly obese get free operations? And so on. The logic of resentment and social sadism is ineluctable once its premises have been allowed to take root.

Worse still, avoiding the difficult issues ultimately reduces the forces available to the Left. If the Left correctly emphasises the working class as the key agency capable of spearheading radical initiatives, the Right attempts to draw a line of antagonism right across the working class – between 'productive', 'hard-working' members of society, and the 'shirkers' and 'skivers'. The fact is that many working class people who are otherwise not right-wing accept this view. And to the extent that they do so, their availability for a genuinely transformative project, one that seeks to redistribute wealth and power in a fundamental way, is limited.

Of course it makes sense to emphasise what is popular about our agenda, but we have to begin to dis-embed those thematics from the dominant neoliberal discourse. For example, popular support for public services is weakened as long as it is tied to an ideology of 'prosperity' and 'wealth creation'. According to this ideology, public spending is purely derivative of the 'real' economy, the private sector. The public sector is only ever parasitic, never productive. This conception underlies the constant mantra of austerians that if there is to be a recovery it must be led by the private sector. Since the 1970s, when public spending seemed to do little but fuel inflation while unemployment continued to rise, the Right has waged a resourceful ideological war to popularize this basic conception. They attacked state spending as a burden on the 'sovereign taxpayer', and a drain on private sector initiative. Their greatest success was in compelling parties of the centre-left to accept their arguments, by defeating the social forces capable of resisting such capitulation. The resulting centre-left parties argued that the only way to pay for and protect public services was to encourage the financial markets to boom, maintain a flexible labour market, and let businesses profit. If the Right continues to win this argument, they'll find it much easier to launch even their most unpopular policies such as cuts and privatisation in the NHS and schools.

The defence of what is good about the status quo, the emphasis on what is popular about our agenda, must somehow be part of a system of articulations that enables us to advocate what is new and radical, and defend what is *not* yet popular. The articulating principles which enable us to do this are vital. If we attempt to ground our agenda in terms of the dominant criteria of *what is good for capitalism*, we cannot win.

And this is where the Left's deepest problem lies: in the deep-rooted crisis of confidence in the possibility of radical alternatives not just to capitalism as such, but to neoliberalism. The Left remains incoherent and fragmented on this point, and has thus far been unable to mediate between its agitation for piecemeal reforms or specific defensive struggles on the one hand, and its most abstract, maximalist agenda ('overthrow capitalism and replace it with something nicer') on the other. In 1970s Britain, the crisis of capitalism was met by a profusion of leftist recommendations for profound transformations, nationalisation of key firms, price controls, democratic planning of the economy, workers' control of at least some industry, and so on. Perhaps the most famous manifesto for an alternative settlement was the Alternative Economic Strategy – which, whatever its limitations, hugely outstrips any rival proposal today.[8] The basic insight underlying this was that if there wasn't a profound and almost irreversible shift of wealth and power away from the rich, akin to 1945, previous gains would be lost.

This is important because any commentary the Left offers in defence of spending or union rights, or to oppose prisonfare or immigration restrictions, must ultimately refer back to a more comprehensive answer to the crisis if it is to be persuasive. For example, consider the challenge: 'How would you fund an expanded welfare state when the economy is so weak and tax revenues are depressed?' The cheap and easy answer is 'borrowing'. But you can only borrow up to a certain point, and it is only viable if it's part of a plausible growth strategy. Another cheap and easy answer: 'tax the rich'. We should certainly do this, but for it to be persuasive it has to be linked to a series of practical means by which the wealth to be taxed is produced. Here, a good starting point might be to say 'nationalise the banks'. This is the biggest weapon in any strategy of redistribution. It is popular, it clarifies certain questions (who the real 'parasites' are for example), achieving it would remove some of the major institutional bases of ruling class power, and it would give any elected government a powerful instrument with which to plan investment.[9]

---

8. A commendable attempt to rethink the Alternative Economic Strategy for today's context is provided by Ed Rooksby, 'An Alternative Economic Strategy', available at edrooksby.wordpress.com, 4 April 2013.

9. This may be off-putting. It may put us in the position of trying to 'manage' capitalism, even if only at a rhetorical level. And it may mean we implicitly accept the idea that there are going to be rich and poor, that for the moment our levelling aspirations can only go so far. But that's politics for you; there are not many successes awaiting 'Beautiful Souls'.

Of course, the problem here is to a significant extent practical. Fine to have manifestos, lovely to have grand synthetic analyses from problem to solution, but ideology that is not materialised in a form of apparatus or organisation is nothing. This raises the question of what types of organisation are suited to the types of political strategy necessary. I will return to this problem in later sections.

State

The dominant role of the state in organising a solution, a 'spatio-temporal fix' to contain capitalism's crisis tendencies, is particularly elevated in the context of austerity. It is especially in this context that the state is increasingly fused with capital, while its democratic functions are eroded. This is one of the key reasons why anti-austerity struggles are predominantly political rather than narrowly economic. A major objective of the Left in the coming years, of whatever variant, must be to significantly transform the state in a democratic direction.

Neoliberals understood the necessity of confronting, attacking and rolling back democratic institutions if their project was to be successful. The power bloc which rules through neoliberalism needed to shift institutional power away from the working class and toward business. And a reorganised neoliberal state could reach well into the 'private sphere', in the spaces where working class self-organisation of various types once existed, and begin to restructure social and political life – largely by 'privatising' it, breaking up collectivist bastions, removing the masses as much as possible from politics, ensuring that more and more areas of social life are structured by competitive market relations. This has deprived the remnants of the Left of the social bases, the organisational and institutional reference points, on which its strategies are based. Indeed, since the state is nothing other than a particular material condensation of the balance of political forces in society, achieving these apparently 'external' effects is precisely one of the means by which the state itself has been transformed. The Left must reach a similar understanding: part of its transformative agenda must in the medium term be to build 'resistances' into the state, spaces where popular interests can be asserted.

Of course, if the state is reduced to a machinery of repression or an instrument of class domination, then such an approach is almost incomprehensible. The best that subaltern forces could achieve for most of the time would be to encircle, limit and contain the state. Having rejected this view, however, it is obvious that we are all to some extent 'inside the state'. This isn't to claim that the state is some sort of totalising, all-encompassing entity, but merely to point out that even if we are not operating within the material spaces of state institutions, our political actions continually traverse the state, affecting the balance of forces within its institutions, and impressing themselves upon its material make-up. It would be hard to imagine what the point of, for example, an anti-war movement would be if this were not the case. Perhaps more importantly, if the state were simply an instrument of domination, it would be difficult to explain how a significant part of the anti-cuts constituency is to be found actually working within the material institutions of the state: the public sector workforce.

A massive expansion of political democracy in as many apparatuses as possible is not just desirable in itself. It would weaken ruling class domination. It would, in a sense, weaken the state itself – precisely in the sense that the Trilateral Commission identified in the 1970s, by inducing a 'crisis of democracy', overloading the state with popular demands and depleting its authority over the popular classes. How is this to be achieved?

In the example of Wisconsin discussed in Chapter 1, I noted the appearance of two contrasting strategies in respect of the developing anti-austerity movement. One, advocated by a small leftist coalition, was based on mobilising workers for the most militant strategy of strikes and all-out opposition to Scott Walker's agenda. The other, advocated by leading union bureaucrats and members of the Democratic opposition, was based on negotiating within the senate chambers while preparing a parliamentary challenge to Walker and the Republicans. The latter strategy was the one that gained the most support, and it failed catastrophically. Looking at the example of Quebec later, I will identify some of the elements of what success looks like. But here one can identify two key tendencies leading to failure: 1) class-mediation, and 2) statism.

In the first instance, class-mediation took the form of the union leadership attempting to strike a deal somewhere between the interests of its membership and the demands of the most right-wing sections of the ruling class. This resulted in failure because it necessitated trying to formulate demands with reference to what the 'progressive' wing of capital, represented by Democrats and the more moderate Republicans, might be willing to accept. When the Right came out in full battle armour, brooking no compromise, ready to dash kith and kin, it found an opposition desperately ceding territory. This was linked to the statist approach, involving deference to the 'rule of law', to parliamentary procedures, and to enlightened administrators.

The strategy of the militant minority, had it prevailed, would have been superior not because it was conducted somehow 'outside' the state, but rather because it sought an alliance of subaltern forces both inside and outside the state organised around a strategy of disruption – strikes, occupations and protests being key. Focused by its demand to repudiate austerity in its entirety, it sought to produce, not a deal, but *ruptures* within the state, such that the balance of forces would shift and this would be reflected in the institutions. It sought, whether or not this was consciously theorised, to *traverse the state*.

This approach, a militant strategy of disruption, does not mean that a parliamentary strategy can be foresworn. It is a longer-term strategy, not one that delivers immediate gratification. But the fact is that the terrain would have been more advantageous to the militant minority if some radical working class forces were represented in office. The fact that the materiality of the state imposes certain limits, that it is heavily pre-structured in favour of the already dominant classes, that it is *selective* in favour of strategies that benefit the capitalist class, does not mean that one can abandon it as a site of contestation.

This is where the parties of the radical left come in. Political parties play a crucial role in organising hegemony, in constructing hegemonic projects through the state. As we saw in the example of Greece, the decomposition of the dominant parties – particularly those traditionally based in the working class – signifies a breakdown of hegemony. But if there is no radical left alternative to occupy the vacated space, the far right are usually ready to begin colonising it.

In Europe, there has been a long-term breakdown of the social democratic parties in the neoliberal period. In several countries – Portugal, France, Greece, Germany – this has resulted in the emergence of more or less successful challengers from the radical left. Syriza, the Greek organisation, has come the closest of all the radical parties to taking office. Far from being the most radical of the Greek left parties, at its core is a historically moderate and pro-European strand, Synaspismós – an offshoot of the many redivisions of Greek communism since 1968. However, it was the turn of Synaspismós toward the social movements and a shift to the left in the early 2000s that led to the formation of Syriza, bringing it into coalition with a range of Maoist, Trotskyist and revolutionary Green parties. It maintained a presence in social movements, and was the only parliamentary party to support the student uprising in 2009, before participating in the 'movement of the squares' in 2011. Finally, its call for a 'united government of the left' to fight austerity policies led to it being propelled to second place in the May 2012 elections. It required a Europe-wide fear campaign on the part of the media and financial institutions to prevent Syriza from gaining office in the follow-up elections in June.

This raised the obvious question of what Syriza could have done once in office. The great virtue of having Syriza elected on a radical agenda – to repeal the Memorandum of Understanding, which gave the banks a bailout in return for deep cuts in the Greek state's budget – was that it amplified popular voices within the state, and disrupted any attempt to build a grand cross-party consensus or 'national unity' government. Syriza, as the main opposition party, refused to have anything to do with a pro-austerity government and left the main capitalist party scrabbling around for allies, eventually making up the numbers with a small 'responsible' left party. It made administering austerity that bit less stable. Not only that, but Syriza could articulate at a national level a radical political agenda that could summon the support of, and cohere, the working class left. Yet once in office, the strongest pressure on a Syriza-led government would undoubtedly have been from opposition parties, state managers, the 'troika', the media and Greek businesses to relent on its anti-Memoran-dum agenda, giving the banks a bailout in return for deep cuts in the Greek state's budget. Certainly, social movements could exert some pressure on Syriza parliamentarians and help stiffen their resolve against media hysteria and EU belligerence. But there was a tremendous fragility about Syriza's position, as there is about all the radical left formations: a structural gap between the support they can achieve in a particular conjuncture and their real social weight.

This is not a factor unique to electoral politics: it is a feature of the period in which the old hegemonic forces of the Left have been in decline, and as yet have not been succeeded by rivals. Linked to certain tendencies in communication technology, particularly the buzz-driven nature of social media as an organising tool, the result is that small groups can often project sudden widespread influence which usually turns out to be short-lived. Nonetheless, in Syriza's case, this meant that any connection to a social base capable of keeping pressure on the organisation was limited. Even without being in office, the quiet, slow rituals and routines of parliamentary politics might be enough to domesticate any parliamentary opposition if it was not integrated into a well-organised social base.

It is essential to get this right, therefore, because the question of governmental power in the context of austerity will come up again. Austerity is fundamentally a political question, pertaining to budgets, laws and the role of the state in securing social reproduction. It is perfectly natural that we should consider the question of what to do about holding office. There are more than enough bad examples to learn from: the fate of the Italian Rifondazione Comunista after its participation in a centre-left government, during which its elected representatives supported privatisation and war, is well known. The successes are largely exceptional – the Chavez experience in Venezuela. But unless the Left simply defaults to backing a social democratic (or just Democratic) lesser evil, with the obvious drawbacks which that entails, it needs to develop a strategy for dealing with the dilemmas of wielding governmental power, and doing so in a way that strengthens the hand of workers and social movements against their class opponents.

However, all of this will be of limited use unless it is linked to another process, which is the flourishing of democracy beyond the state. A beginning of this process was signified by the 'movement of the squares' and the Occupy movements. These have worked variously as a type of direct action and direct democracy; a protest and a pedagogical space; and a temporary tactical base from which to plan actions of solidarity and disruption. But they have been limited by the fact that the spaces they have taken are, while visible, strategically marginal, by the fact that those involved wield little potential disruptive power, and by the fact that their actions were eventually outmanoeuvred by state power.

It was on a cold Autumn day that I visited the Occupy camp in London on some journalistic pretext.[10] It was dress-down Monday for the filth, who had abandoned their tooled up, combative posture from the previous weekend, and were taking a more relaxed approach to policing the occupation zone outside St Paul's cathedral. The occupation, poised at the centre of the mean square mile, was intended to distress and mildly inconvenience the rich. It also made excellent propaganda.

The architecture of the occupation was deceptively simple: it looked like a colony of sleeping tents draped with banners and bristling with painted placards. Upon the main banner was inscribed 'Capitalism IS Crisis'. On some railings, a more optimistic sentiment was offered: 'We Are the 99%'. But this was to ignore the free-food stand, the small generator powering 'media tech', the media centre where one could usually find someone to answer questions, the information point, the first-aid area, the 'surplus' tent where people were invited to donate useful goods, the dish-washing facility, the art corner where people made the many signs that apprised well-heeled passers-by, and the regular garbage collection service. Since the police removed the toilet facilities on the pretext of 'cleaning' them, and did not replace them, the occupiers had to send out teams to visit local businesses and work out arrangements with them. The entire infrastructure was run by the occupiers.

This was a striking shift from what had gone on before. Britain, in the autumn of 2010, was entropic. There was a state of numb resignation. Few outside the gilded elites in the City and the senior

---

10. I reported on this in full on my blog. See 'Visiting Occupy London', *Lenin's Tomb*, 17 October 2011, available at www.leninology.com.

civil service really wanted what had happened – this government, with this programme. There were morbid symptoms everywhere: a flimsy coalition, spectacular affluence at the top without growth, the profusion of 'third sector' policy sound-bites as the dominant parties sought a happy thematic medium between state failure and market failure, the hybridisation of the major parties as Red Tories and Blue Labourites sought to find just the right electoral synthesis to preserve their respective parties' longevities.

The coalition government itself was the result of a peculiar conjunction of factors – the secular decline of Conservatism; the utter enervation of New Labour; a brief, sputtering 'Cleggasm', in which the Liberal Democrats benefited from a temporary rush to 'honest' middle-of-the-road government among a section of the voting population; a sustained campaign by stock market investors to 'vote' for a Liberal-Tory coalition once the results came through; and an ad hoc civil service set of rules for negotiations.

Clegg was the beneficiary of a diffuse spectacle, one composed of memes, trending topics, 'likes' and retweets. Labour, having shed its austere Brownness, had chosen for its leader someone whose two major appealing characteristics were that he wasn't his brother, and no one knew who he was. It transpired that he was a physically graceless, uncharismatic twin of his brother. The Tories were the beneficiaries of the worst of popular culture. TV presenter Jeremy Kyle, the overseer of a sadism spectacle saturated with the country's provincial prejudices and class resentments, had been spotted at the Conservative Party conference sitting next to Chancellor George Osborne, himself the purveyor of a kind of sado-liberalism. Occasionally, there was a slightly morbid fascination with what didn't happen – where were all the strikes and protests?

The answer was brisk: a student movement that produced ripples of euphoric radicalisation for the several weeks it took the government to pass a bill trebling tuition fees and the police to beat and demoralise the opposition. And then, the *annus mirabilus* of 2011 – with revolts spreading from Egypt to Greece, the Occupy movement and *indignados*, and great popular rebellions against austerity measures – seemed to confirm that the torpor was at an end. The sectional trade union responses to austerity seemed to be fusing, unevenly, with a wider political response. It was like, someone said, coming out of depression.

The organisational inspiration for the Occupy movement came, to a large extent, from Tahrir Square. Here, for example, are some of the features of the revolutionary movement that overthrew Mubarak. First of all, an anti-dictatorship alliance forged through a decade of anti-war activism, electoral initiatives and labour struggles, took over a nominally public space which the state wished to exclude them from, Tahrir Square. Having taken it over, and affirmed that they wouldn't simply go home at the end of the day, they saw off wave after wave of assault on the protests, from police and plain-clothes thugs. They set up committees to keep watch for government men. They set up barricades, and routine ID checks for everyone attempting to enter the square. They set up a network of tents for people to sleep in – it was freezing overnight, so some of them jogged round the square to get their temperature up. There were toilet arrangements – no small logistical matter when there were routinely hundreds of thousands of people occupying the capital's main intersection. They rigged up street lamps to provide electricity. They set up garbage collection, medical stops – they occupied a well-known fast-food outlet and turned it into somewhere that people beaten or shot at by police could get treated.

In brief, they set up a city within a city, and collectively coped with many more challenges than the average city would have to face in an average day. There was of course commerce, people hawking food and cigarettes, confident that the whole system of exchange wasn't being overthrown. Yet, far more of their actions were driven by solidarity, collective decision-making, and democratic delegation, than is ever usual for a city. Tahrir Square was the beginnings of a commune. Beyond that spectacular exercise in the capital, the labour movement that had been kicking since the 2006 strikes in Mahalla was doing something that labour movements usually don't do. It was starting to strike to demand a change in management. It was striking over the exercise of authority. This had happened in Tunisia, and usually it was because the CEO was some ruling party stooge. But it was the people who normally have no say in the running of the company seeking to exercise a sort of limited franchise. They did not seek to replace the management of the company with themselves, which would have been the ultimate statement of their confidence in their ability to rule themselves. But they were trying to have a say, and usually succeeded in that. And when the government withdrew the police from local communities and encouraged looting and thuggish behaviour, the people – instead of panicking, and deciding 'we can't do without the police after all, please send the uniformed thugs back in Mr Mubarak' – organised self-defence committees. Just as in Tahrir, they set up checkpoints, ID checks, and made decisions about how their community would be run.

These successful experiments in self-government were only germinal. They were not linked to a radical political agenda – the only shared goal was deposing a dictator. But in this respect, they did something that revolutionary movements usually find themselves compelled to do: establish autonomous centres of legitimate authority outside and against the state. In so doing, of course, they exerted effects within the state, exacerbating divisions in the power bloc, ultimately isolating the dictatorship and causing the breakdown of its key political and repressive apparatuses. But, manifestly, theirs was not a statist approach, deferring to wise heads within the state, bowing to 'law and order', waiting for the parliamentary process to absorb and deal with their grievances.

Such experiments rarely take off in parliamentary-democratic states, and the Occupy movement was never able to establish more than a network of makeshift proto-communes. Ideologically speaking, the occupiers inhabited an unstable continuum that might be called 'anarcho-reformism'. There was a certain anarchist suspicion of traditional parties, traditional institutional politics, even the Left–Right divide as conventionally understood. There was an emphasis on democratic process and horizontal decision-making taken from the autonomist wing of the anticapitalist movement. I asked occupiers what they sought to achieve in the end, how they would seriously challenge the dominance of the rich. 'We're on day three', I was told. 'The whole point of consensus decision-making is that we don't know what the answer is, and that we have to come to that answer through a process which is inclusive, which is democratic.'

The sense in which the movement was 'reformist', however, was in its ambitions for change:

> What we have agreed, is that the current system is not working and that it needs change. And we have some suggestions for that, which include that idea that we need regulators that are truly independent from the institutions which they regulate, that we need government that works for people not the corporations, and that we put people before profits.

But this was a 'reformism' radicalising in the direction of an anti-systemic stance. The end of ensuring that the 'world's resources' 'go towards caring for people and the planet, not the military, corporate profits or the rich' may not have been precise, but realistically the realisation of such a goal implied a challenge to capitalism. It is just that the lack of ideological and political cohesion rendered it less likely that this could ultimately be materialised.

Eventually, not being nourished by wider social and industrial disruption, not being situated in strategically privileged sites where the social order is reproduced, and comprising marginal youths, students and others with little social power, the Occupy movement was taken apart by attrition and police action. By the end of 2011, the revolt was at an end, leaving only a few embers to sift through. The key lesson I would invite readers to draw from this is that there is no short-cut to success: the infrastructure of popular self-organisation must be reconstructed, and this will take time.

Nonetheless, the Occupy movement was a learning process which had radicalising effects and helped weaken the Right. Its call to unite the 99% against the 1% put class, and class power, on the agenda. Its focus on financial capital directed popular resentment against the most powerful sectors of the ruling class. Its emphasis on democracy recorded exactly what was being eroded under neoliberalism – as David Graeber contended, in such times 'any awakening of the democratic impulse can only be a revolutionary urge'.[11] And it pointed

---

11. David Graeber, *The Democracy Project: A History, A Crisis, A Movement*, Penguin, 2013, Kindle edition, loc. 171.

to a necessary component of any radical strategy: the development of organisation 'from below', of self-management, of tenants' groups, workers' committees, a profusion of democratic organisations through which people try to solve their problems collectively.

Three types of action thus comprise what Charles Tilly would call an emerging 'repertoire of contention':[12] strikes and other trade union responses to austerity; radical social movement responses; and parliamentary intervention to break open the traditional social democratic monopoly over the working class vote, change the debate in the media, and establish 'resistances' within the state. The key strategic question posed by this brief upsurge of radical democracy is how to effectively link these forms of action through the appropriate organisational forms and political idioms.

Class

Austerity is a class strategy. But classes, in themselves, do nothing. There must be certain forms of class leadership to argue for certain types of strategy or goals, and implement them.

Austerity is not simply a get-rich-quick scheme for the bankers. The rich get rich to the extent that capitalism grows, and therefore austerity is part of a long-term growth strategy (even if growth is suppressed in the short term), an attempt to reorganise production, to alter the configuration of power, and to change the social compact in order to make investment profitable. This is organised not by the capitalist class in itself, which is too divided by ruthless competition and divergences of short-term interest to coalesce for very long, but by a power bloc under the dominance of financial capital. This power bloc, I have suggested, comprises the higher sections of finance, manufacturing and services capital, linked by 'interlocking directorates' that permit its members to gain a class-wide purview and coalesce on political activism.[13] Further, I have argued that this

---

12. Charles Tilly, *Regimes and Repertoires*, University of Chicago Press, Chicago and London, 2006.

13. For a detailed empirical discussion, see Useem, *The Inner Circle: Large Corporations and the Rise of Business Political Activity in the US and UK*.

power bloc was connected to and dominated the state not only in indirect ways – the 'homeostatic' mechanism according to which states must respond to capitalist interests in order to produce the growth which secures their ability to govern – but through direct institutional mechanisms where their power is concentrated.[14]

If this account is accepted, at least provisionally, then the question arises as to how an opposing class strategy might be developed and implemented. After all, *the unity of classes can in no way be assumed or taken for granted*; it has to be actively constructed, organised through a set of apparatuses and ideologies. We have already seen the inadequacy of traditional apparatuses, those of social democracy. In the past, the left-of-social-democracy Left has looked to trade unions as the locus where a collective working class strategy might be developed. But, of course, while trade unions are mass organisations with enormous potential power, they are organised under bureaucracies which tend toward ineffectual conservatism and conciliation. This is particularly true in an era in which attacks on union militancy has resulted in a steady shift of power to the bureaucracies.

Further, there are differences among workers which tend to militate against a shared outlook, even among those workers who are organised in unions. For this reason, the class-oriented Left has looked to the 'rank and file' in unions as the basis for a militant socialist political movement. In its Leninist declination, this would take the form of a fusion between a revolutionary socialist party and the most radical sections of the working class. This would be the 'vanguard', a mass organisation, quite unlike the 57 varieties of 'vanguard party' that exist in the world today. However, this 'rank and file' no longer exists in any meaningful sense.

---

14. I may be accused by some of describing a 'conspiracy' here. However, effective class political action need not – indeed, logically could not – be a conspiracy. In fact much of what I'm describing takes place 'openly', in newspapers, think-tanks, party-political discourse, government white papers, and so on. If some of these things are obscure it is not mainly because of official secrecy or plotting in darkened rooms. Rather, as I have said, ideology saturates both elite and popular perceptions of how power works.

Not only that, but the unions are growing ever more narrow relative to the working class as a whole. Even in Britain, where the trade union movement still includes some 6.5 million members as of 2013, the stratification of the working class in the neoliberal era means that the conditions of unionised workers are increasingly unlike those of other workers.[15] Non-unionised workers work more hours, for on average less pay, with less job security, than unionised workers. Even as the 'union premium' has been substantially eroded through austerity, the trend is not toward an equalisation of conditions but merely new forms of stratification.

This poses two types of problem. In the long term, there is a need for a 'new unionism', the extension of trade unions into those nine out of ten private sector workforces which have no union representation. This is no easy matter when so many of the workforces that need unions the most are least susceptible to unionisation. Consider the paradigmatic workplace of the 2000s: the call centre. Here, working environments are often small, and out of the way. Generally speaking there is a high turnover of staff, workers are employed on a casual, temporary and part-time basis, and there are a large number of employees on the roster who have either long since moved on to new employment or are only rarely seen. Forming the relationships necessary to build support for unionisation, then organising a ballot of all employees, is extremely difficult in such circumstances.

In brief, it seems to me that the only plausible basis upon which a 'new unionism' could be constructed is through a fusion of Social Movement Unionism and Community Unionism. In the first instance, organising union activity on the basis of relevant political issues is both pertinent to the wider interests of members and a way of being in reach of the many working class people who are politicised but have never been in a union. In the second instance, there are many issues which affect working class people, from tenancy rights to energy prices. Community Unionism allows people to join a union as community members, whereby they can gain support for their particular needs and struggles in exchange for participation and a

---

15. On stratification, see Richard Seymour, 'Hovis's Zero-hours Strike and the Wrong Way to Share Out Work', *The Guardian*, 22 August 2013.

financial contribution. Rather than starting by building branches in a multitude of small, dispersed workplaces, where the bargaining power of workers is relatively weak, one can start to reconstitute a trade union presence and political identity by setting up shop in town centres and communities, offering people free assistance and the opportunity to be members of a union that they might otherwise never be in contact with. This sort of outreach and mobilisation was, for example, partly the basis of the broad anti-privatisation coalition that was assembled in Bolivia before 2001.[16]

In the short term, however, there is a need to assemble the actually existing heterogeneous class forces into an effective anti-austerity alliance, which will have to become urgently effective. This is where the recomposition of the working class poses other problems. The 'working class' is, as we have seen, not a fixed entity. The shift to a feminised, better educated workforce; the 'tertiarisation' of unions (meaning they are increasingly situated in public service occupations); the growth of a student workforce and of precarious labour, means that the language of class that once made sense is harder to apply. The strategies and tactics devised in the 1970s, more so those concocted in the 1920s and 1930s, will have limited purchase today. And this is where the question of political identities and their relationship to class formation is critical. A certain emerging type of criticism of the contemporary Left from within is that it has spent too much time on trendy 'identitarian' concerns, from anti-racism to Gaza, and not enough time focusing on class.

Owen Jones, in his justly popular book *Chavs*, argues that 30 years of defeats for the labour movement have resulted in a 'shift away from class politics towards identity politics'. Far from dismissing the issues he characterises as 'identity politics' – the 'exceptionally important' 'struggles for the emancipation of women, gays and ethnic minorities' – he nonetheless is concerned that they have

---

16. On this, see David McNally, 'Radical Democracy and Popular Power: Thinking About New Socialisms for the 21st Century', *Varieties of Socialism, Varieties of Approaches*, Carleton University, 5 March 2011, available at www.vimeo.com.

been coopted and used to displace class.[17] While it is not difficult to see what he is getting at, it is worth noting that the class politics he advocates – for example, community mobilisations over housing – are *inextricable* from a politics of identity and the 'local'. Moreover, there is simply no way to discuss class without also talking about the way in which it is structured by gender, race and so on. They are not competing, but contiguous issues.

This means we have to break with a limiting assumption about identity. It is often assumed that identity politics is a form of 'particularism' whose political radius extends no wider than the specific group or subculture identified – black gay women for example. Yet identity is a much more slippery concept than this would imply. It is not distinguished only by its affirmation of the culturally or politically proximate, but also by the process of identification which involves the perception of, for example, shared interests. And interests are interesting things: they can be expansive, or narrow; inclusive, or aloof. Identity politics is a 'politics of location', certainly. But where one is situated in the social formation has consequences for how far one can see. Such is the basic proposition of the feminist notion of 'intersectionality'.[18]

The multiplication of lines of antagonism in contemporary capitalism, and the politicisation of growing areas of life, from childbirth to the environment to policing, need not constitute an unwelcome narrowing of horizons, a reduction of politics to competing particularisms. On the contrary, the forces that emerge to support any given oppositional movement will generally come from some identity-position, and usually more than one given that lines of antagonism intersect and the fields of politicisation overlap. It is no accident that the effects of austerity are so racially laden, and so gender laden. For example, in so far as the wider social reproduction

---

17. Owen Jones, *Chavs: The Demonization of the Working Class*, Verso, London and New York, 2012, p. 255.
18. Kimberle Crenshaw, 'Mapping the Margins: Intersectionality, Identity Politics, and Violence Against Women of Color', *Stanford Law Review* 43:6, 1991, pp. 1241–99; Patricia Hill Collins, *Black Feminist Thought: Knowledge, Consciousness, and the Politics of Empowerment*, Routledge, New York, 1991.

of capitalism is dependent upon work that is unwaged and disproportionately carried out by women,[19] the question of the social wage – the remuneration handed out by the state in the form of benefits – is necessarily gendered.

As Judith Butler has argued, there are therefore two ways that the Left can respond to this.[20] It can attempt to construct a form of political unity based on exclusions – a unity which suppresses or demotes issues that are 'merely cultural' in the name of 'class'. But this sort of class politics will be implicitly white, male and metropolitan. And it will not work; the genie will not go back into the bottle. Or it can try to construct a *unity in difference*, negotiating between identities because it acknowledges these as arising from material issues of oppression and injustice that are no less important than those of class injustice.

One of the most telling, and challenging, symptoms of class recomposition and its effects is the emerging concept of 'the precariat'.[21] The very real spread of precarity and insecurity in the workforce raises issues of class unity and identification which cannot be avoided by simply denying any real changes have taken place.

Precarity is, in and of itself, nothing new. 'Dock labouring is at all times a precarious and uncertain mode of living', a dock worker recounted in 1882. 'The supply of workmen in Liverpool always greatly exceeds the demand and the consequence is that the average earnings the year round do not exceed four days, or 18s per week.'[22] The agrarian proletariat of early modern England was just as vulnerable to fluctuating demand for labour, requiring constant intervention by the Tudor state to prevent a catastrophic

---

19. On this, Silvia Federici's *Revolution at Point Zero* is essential reading.
20. Judith Butler, 'Merely Cultural', *New Left Review* I/227, January–February 1998.
21. On this, see Richard Seymour, 'We Are All Precarious – On the Concept of the "Precariat" and its Misuses', *New Left Project*, 10 February 2012; the standard account, which I find lacking, is Guy Standing, *The Precariat: The New Dangerous Class*, Bloomsbury, London, 2011.
22. 'The Life of a Dock Labourer 1882', from *Liverpool Mercury*, December 1882, republished at www.old-merseytimes.co.uk.

population loss. The cotton spinners of the early industrial age were regularly out of work, searching for errands to run, traders to serve, sundry items to sell: patching together a living from the flotsam of urban capitalism. As old as capitalism, such insecurity has always characterised substantial margins of the economy, with women and the racially oppressed carrying out the bulk of precarious work.

A widespread intuition, however, is that we are in a qualitatively new phase of development, in which the marginal has become the core – encompassing, according to some estimates, perhaps as many as a quarter of all workers. Denoted by a family of terms such as 'McJobs', 'junk jobs', 'flexiworking', and so on, this line of thinking is based upon the transformation of labour markets by the technological, spatial and organisational re-structuring of capitalism.

In the Fordist model of capitalism pioneered in the early twentieth century, managers would use various mechanisms to retain a stable, well-regulated labour force. 'Scientific management' along Taylorist lines would increase the productivity of workers, while ensuring their subordination to management, by breaking up work processes into a set of discrete, calculable tasks. Skill was thus taken, as much as possible, off the 'shop floor', and hived off into managerial offices. The expertise of the craft worker was replaced by the predictable, routinised tasks of the industrial worker. This is the basis for the old division between mental and manual labour, which is really a division between executive and menial labour. Just as importantly, firms would use a combination of material inducements, ideological appeals, bargaining mechanisms, and direct intervention in the family life of workers, to cultivate corporate loyalty and cohesion. Ford himself pointed out that paying a relatively 'high wage' could save a great deal of money in the long term by reducing labour turnover and keeping productivity high. Though initially hostile to unions, in the Cold War period Fordist producers learned to incorporate organised labour as a partner in constantly improving productivity.

The break-up of this corporatist system as a result of the long, turbulent crisis of the 1970s resulted in a fundamental transformation of work. Post-Fordist capitalism, it is argued, has increasingly dispensed with long-term employment, as managers and administrators have sought to make production more flexible.[23] Particularly in the service sector, from hotels and catering to cleaning and low-grade office jobs, more and more tasks are 'contracted out' to firms that hire workers on a casual and temporary basis. Positions once occupied by full-time workers are taken by temps for months at a time.

This process is creating a dynamically expanding stratum of workers who, while often well educated, are insecure, lack prospects, and form transient modes of existence out of fragmentary work and social lives. With little corporate loyalty, and only light group solidarity among themselves, this is a highly individualistic class-in-the-making. Their sociality, at least in the core capitalist economies, takes the form of 'networks', predicated on social media, rather than the 'communities' of outmoded forms of working class life. It is they who have rebelled, in the anticapitalist protests, the student protests, and the occupations. This is the 'precariat'.

There have been empirically robust challenges to this conceit,[24] pointing to the fact that the emphasis on non-standard employment as the basis for the precariat unhelpfully bundles into a single category diverse types of labour. All that unites them is what they are not (viz. 'standard'). In so far as temporary employment is important, it has risen drastically in some cases, but on average rose by only 2 per cent across OECD economies between 1985 and 2004. Job tenure varied, but on average some 42 per cent of workers were employed at the same firm for a year or more. Other forms of non-standard employment overlap only weakly with temp-work patterns. Flexible employment may, for example, be manifest due to 'family-friendly' legislation, or seasonal patterns, or industry-specific need for shift-work.[25]

This is hardly to deny real changes in employment. The return of mass unemployment,[26] the growth of part-time work and under-

---

23. On post-Fordism, see Scott Lash and John Urry, *The End of Organized Capitalism*, Polity Press, Cambridge, 1987.

24. See Kevin Doogan, *New Capitalism?: The Transformation of Work*, Polity Press, Cambridge, 2009.

25. See ibid., Chapter 7.

26. A pattern reinforced by institutional commitment to the doctrine of a non-accelerating inflation rate of unemployment (or NAIRU).

employment, the emergence of vast pools of precarious migrant workers,[27] and the rise of student labour are all arguably manifestations of precarity. These patterns are racialised and gendered, and linked to forms of segregation, ghettoisation, 'workfare' and 'prisonfare'. Globally, moreover, they are linked to the imperialist structure of accumulation, as the greatest degrees of precarity are found in those parts of the planet subject to episodes of plunder punctuated by malign neglect.[28] This is to say nothing of the growing numbers of unemployed and under-employed slum-dwellers, an effect of neoliberal urbanisation in developing capitalist economies.[29]

So, even if the 'precariat' doesn't really resemble a new social class,[30] the concept is clearly addressing real changes in class formation. I suggest that it is a kind of populist interpellation which operates on a real, critical antagonism in today's capitalism. To explain the terminology a little: 'interpellation' refers to the way in which ideology constitutes one as a subject, a process of 'subjectification'. When one heeds the 'call' of the Christian faith, for example, one is 'interpellated' by it, becoming in the process a 'believing subject'. A populist interpellation involves popular-democratic ideology, subjectifying one as a member of 'the people' in opposition to the power bloc (however the latter is construed).

The antagonism on which this populist interpellation works arises over the forced precariousness of labour. The neoliberal era, which

---

27. According to David McNally, three quarters of China's manufacturing jobs are filled by migrant workers who have no access to social services or schools. McNally, *Global Slump*, p. 52.

28. The waged and salaried comprise 84% of the employment total in the 'developed countries' (the EU, US, Japan, Canada, Australia, etc.), in contrast to sub-Saharan Africa, where the waged and salaried comprise a mere 23%, with the largest chunk, 49%, being self-employed. The latter are largely denied the forms of collective organisation that waged and salaried workers can muster in defence of jobs, pay and conditions. See Goran Therborn, *The World: A Beginner's Guide*, Polity, Cambridge, 2010, for statistics.

29. Mike Davis, *Planet of Slums*, Verso, London and New York, 2007.

30. Notably, the precariat possesses no intrinsic relations to other social classes, and is defined by no specific mechanisms of self-reproduction.

has had to be jump-started by austerity, has introduced particular forms of precarity linked to financialisation and unemployment; the current austerity project, through which neoliberalism is to be deepened and entrenched, will spread that insecurity further up the chain of classes and strata, leaving only a minority relatively secure. This is what the language of precarity is addressing.

Thus, it seems to me that in the short term we are in the business of trying to stitch together an alliance of the working majority, 'the 99%', on the basis of reconciling diverse and sometimes antagonistic subject-positions. We need an institutional format that can accommodate and include such diverse interests. Not only that, but it must be capable of federating such diverse and relatively 'spontaneous' struggles as emerge, amplifying them and linking them to others while condensing them in a political platform that is broadly accepted. It must, finally, access the strengths, the forms of leverage that multiple groups can exercise beyond the obvious strike actions. These are best comprehended in terms of Frances Fox Piven's notion of 'disruptive power':[31] the fact that poor and subaltern forces contribute to the reproduction of the system, cooperating in it, and can withdraw that cooperation just as workers can withdraw their labour power.

That format is neither the radical left party nor the trade union, but the social movement. The main elements of a social movement, its combination of different types of collective action, publicity and claims on targeted authorities,[32] can be put to work in a way that provides a nourishing milieu and terrain in which trade unions and parties of the radical left can intersect and coordinate. The institutional framework must, if it is to be effective, seek to build on the achievements of the Spanish *indignados* and Occupy in

---

31. Frances Fox Piven, *Challenging Authority: How Ordinary People Change America*, Rowman & Littlefield Publishers Inc., Lanham MD, 2006.

32. 'As it developed in the West after 1750, the social movement emerged from an innovative, consequential synthesis of three elements:

    1. a sustained, organized public effort making collective claims on target authorities (let us call it a campaign);

establishing protocols for direct democracy. Anything less will be totally counterproductive.

In the final example of this book, I want to look at a rare success for an anti-austerity movement, that of the students' movement in Quebec.

Example 5: A Rare Success in Quebec

No political success is ever complete, or anything other than provisional. But what the student movement and its allies achieved in Quebec was a rare and outstanding victory against an austerity project. The government, wielding the hatchet in the one hand and the police baton in the other, had gone to war against the students, and then gone to the polls on a 'law and order' platform. It lost both fights.

Students in Quebec inhabit militant traditions inherited from the 'quiet revolution' of the 1960s,[33] when the province's francophone majority pushed for full access to higher education as part of a series of sweeping reforms. This inaugurated a student movement, whose signature was the mass student strike. Each time a government attempted to drive up tuition fees, the students walked out – and

---

2. employment of combinations from among the following forms of political action: creation of special-purpose associations and coalitions, public meetings, solemn processions, vigils, rallies, demonstrations, petition drives, statements to and in public media, and pamphleteering (call the variable ensemble of performances the social movement repertoire); and

3. participants' concerted public representations of WUNC: worthiness, unity, numbers, and commitment on the part of themselves and/or their constituencies (call them WUNC displays).' Charles Tilly, *Social Movements: 1768–2004*, Paradigm Publishers, Boulder & London, 2004, pp. 3–4.

33. For background on the Canadian student movement of the 1960s, see Chris Hurl and Kevin Walby, 'We are the Student Movement?: Remembering the Rise and Fall of the Canadian Union of Students, 1965–1969', *Upping the Anti* 9, 2009.

most of the time, they won. As a result, there is a thriving democratic culture among Quebec's students.

The organisational structure of the student unions is far closer to that of a trade union than the sort of lobby organisation that the British National Union of Students is morphing into. As one participant in that movement explained:

> The first thing to understand is that the Québec student movement is organized around a trade union model. Everyone is a member of the union and pays dues, and there is a closed shop; by law you have to certify a student union in Québec. So student unions are not just action groups. This organizational model forms the basis for a fairly stable and institutionalized movement which gives the student union financial autonomy, and provides the basis for certain forms of direct democracy.[34]

When the Liberal government of Jean Charest sought to increase tuition fees by 75 per cent in 2012, it was the student organisations that led a popular, broad coalition against the government. The government, adopting a militant posture, had refused to negotiate with the student organisations. As a result, in February 2012, the students called for a strike, and a boycott of classes began.[35] Adopting the red square which had been the symbol of the last militant student protest in Quebec in 2005, they sought to expand their movement and its repertoires well beyond just what students by themselves could accomplish.

The radical spearhead of the movement was the Coalition Large de l'Association pour une Solidarité Syndicale Étudiante, or Classe. Emerging from a decade of left-wing student unionism, Classe was explicitly formed in December 2011 to build a students' strike to stop the fees rise. Going further than most student bodies, it demanded the cancellation of all tuition fees, to be paid for by a tax on banks. This

---

34. Aidan Conway, 'The Strike of the General Assembly: An Interview with Nicolas Phebus', *Upping The Anti* 2, 2005.

35. Henry A. Giroux, 'Days of Rage: The Quebec Student Protest Movement and the New Social Awakening', *Truthout*, 28 August 2012.

stance was very popular, and the group eventually incorporated 65 local affiliates and 100,000 members comprising the most politicised and activist core of the province's 400,000 strong student body.

Beginning with a series of small-scale disruptive actions – a sit-in at a government office, a road blockade – the first major protest took place on 22nd March 2012 in downtown Montreal. This rapidly escalated into mass protests involving hundreds of thousands.[36] General assemblies of students were held across Quebec to discuss and implement a strike. This meant boycotting and picketing classes, and at their height the strikes achieved the support of 300,000 students.

The structures of direct democracy built on campuses sustained the momentum behind the strikes, enabling students to meet, discuss and make decisions on a regular basis. Each month, the movement called a mass mobilisation, with tens of thousands of students gathering in the Place du Canada in Montreal. But there was also a heated debate over the strategy and goals of the movement. It wasn't enough to keep the momentum going. In addition to the strikes, radical students sought to disrupt the smooth functioning of the economy and the government, carrying out blockades and occupations of banks and government buildings.

Importantly, the student leadership refused to be divided. When the government excluded Classe from negotiations, in the hope of engaging the more moderate student federations in a compromise, the latter walked out. But students also reached out to the labour movement. Theirs was a class issue, they insisted, and Classe called for a 'social strike' of both students and workers. They consciously sought alliances with Rio Tinto workers locked out of their jobs,[37] public sector workers facing cuts, campaigns against increased fees for healthcare, and local resistance to the government's attempts to turn over northern resources to the mining industry. Neighbourhood protests – the notorious 'casserole' protests involving residents banging pots and pans – became a regular occurrence. A number

---

36. Judy Rebick, 'Maple Spring: Quebec Students Protest Tuition Hikes in Massive Numbers', *rabble.ca*, 22 March 2012.

37. Jesse McLaren, 'Photo Essay: Global Day of Action in Alma, Quebec', *rabble.ca*, 2 April 2012.

of union federations passed motions for strike action, though in the event the resistance from union leaders was too strong, and the labour militants too weak, to make it happen.

Repression was also far less effectual in these circumstances. The police used thousands of arrests and severely violent tactics to try to disrupt the protests. The most violent suppression took place on 4th May in Victoriaville, when police used gas, chemical agents and plastic bullets against protesters.[38] Inevitably, the media reporting of this suppression took the form of describing 'violent clashes', and suggesting that it was the protest that had 'turned violent', and not the counter-protest mobilised by police.[39]

Eventually, the government reached for emergency legislation to hammer the strike: Bill 78. The law, passed on 18th May 2012 by Liberals with the support of the province's employers,[40] banned demonstrations within 50 metres of a college or university. It insisted that protests of 50 or more people must submit their intended route to police eight hours in advance. Police were empowered to change the planned route or location, and it was the responsibility of protest organisers to inform participants. And the law imposed severe fines on those who did not comply – protest organisers could be severely penalised, up to $125,000 for student unions, if individual protesters did not obey. This was a law designed to make student strikes impossible; it was a ban.

But the protests continued in defiance of the laws. A major protest on 22nd May was organised specifically to repudiate the law, in what was a mass act of civil disobedience. Over 400,000 participated and, although almost a thousand protesters were arrested, it was obvious that the state was unable to muster sufficient forces to shut down a

38. An inquiry, appointed under pressure from the Left, has begun to record some of these facts. See Peter Rakobowchuk and Julien Arsenault, 'Hearings into Quebec's 2012 Student Protests Begin', *The Canadian Press*, 23 September 2013.

39. See, for example, Monique Muise and Christopher Curtis, 'Protest at Quebec Liberal Party Convention Turns Violent', *National Post*, 5 May 2012.

40. For employers' reactions, see 'Bill 78 – Quebec Employers Council President Offers Comments', *CNW Telbec*, 18 May 2012.

march of this size. When police demanded a map of the march route, the protesters supplied a route outline that looked decidedly like a fist holding a middle finger aloft.[41]

In tandem with the legal-repressive tactic, though, Charest sought to gain some democratic legitimacy for what he was doing. He called a general election for 4th September, timed to coincide with the coming into effect of most of the anti-student-strike legislation in Bill 78. A combination of a legislative victory and a political victory would be necessary and perhaps sufficient to finish off the student movement.[42]

In fact, Charest and the Liberals lost, as their support plummeted by ten percentage points. Partly this was a simple collapse of confidence among Liberal voters in the political leadership: many of the lost votes were picked up by a centre-right alternative, the Coalition Avenir Québec. The opposition Parti Québécois won the election despite seeing its overall vote share decline, and the leftist party, Québec solidaire, increased its share of the vote to over 6 per cent, becoming the fourth parliamentary party and gaining an extra parliamentary seat. On coming to power, the new PQ government announced a freeze on tuition fee hikes and subsequently repealed the most punitive sections of Bill 78.

This success was, as indicated, limited and provisional. The goal of free tuition was not attained, and the new government eventually opted for a strategy of indexing tuition fees to the cost of living, thus leading to new rises and provoking new protests.[43] Nonetheless, it *was* a victory. The elements going into this success cannot simply be packaged and exported to contexts outside of Quebec. The long traditions of student militancy and self-organisation, the

---

41. 'Maple Spring: Nearly 1,000 Arrested as Mass Quebec Student Strike Passes 100th Day', *Democracy Now*, 25 May 2012; Adam Taylor, 'Here's What Montreal's Students Protesters Responded With When Cops Asked To See Their March Route', *Business Insider*, 24 May 2012.

42. See Benoit Renaud, 'Inside the Quebec Election, a View From the Left', *Socialist.ca*, 5 October 2012.

43. Stephen Petrina, 'Quebec Students Back in Streets Protesting Tuition Hikes', *Workplace Blog*, 27 March 2013.

deeply entrenched social democratic attitudes linked to Quebecois nationalism,[44] and the profound strategic miscalculations of the Charest government are not easy to translate into other situations. This is partially why any anti-austerity strategy has to include an element of long-range reconstruction, whereby a grassroots democratic infrastructure and militant left-wing culture can be implanted and cultivated over a generation.

Nonetheless, there seem to be a number of replicable strategic and tactical lessons. In the first instance, the most radical of the Quebec students – represented by the organisation CLASSE, who were able to play a leading role – did not seek to narrowly limit their goals in the misplaced belief that they would gain more sympathy by doing so. They understood the necessity of creating a 'chain of equivalents' linking their struggle to the issues facing other sectors of society. Starting from the perspective of class, they deployed a leftist ideology that resonated with traditionally social democratic views, and assembled a 'system of alliances' that at times looked something like 'the 99%'. It was not necessary in this case that there should be one formally instituted 'united front', but the *de facto* unity of diverse organisations and constituencies was essential.

Second, the movement adopted a *militant* rather than *parliamentarist* strategy. Inevitably, fighting and winning tactical battles on the parliamentary terrain was a crucial part of their victory. The existence of a radical left, anti-neoliberal party, Québec solidaire, helped polarise the parliamentary battle more to the left than would have otherwise been the case. To this extent, the battle was fought both inside and outside the state. But the starting point for the protesters was to work on the terrains where they were strongest, not where they had least strategic advantage, and this meant emphasising their disruptive capacity. This they did, in disregard for the inevitable ideological and repressive offensives against them. In so doing, they successfully shifted the balance of forces within the state, dividing and defeating their most belligerent opponents.

---

44. On the complexities of Quebecois nationalism and the state's neoliberal accumulation strategy, see Cory Brad, *Neoliberalism and National Culture: State-Building and Legitimacy in Canada and Quebec*, Haymarket Books, Chicago, 2013.

Third, they did not defer to 'law and order', but actively deployed a *civil disobedience* model of action when the law was deployed against them. This was made easier due to the direct-democratic aspects of student organising in Quebec. The more hierarchical and top-down the model of organising, the easier it is for a leadership at some remove from the base to limit the spontaneity and militancy of the movement.[45] In the end, their political success in organising a broad movement prevailed over the edge that the state had in terms of coercion and force.

*   *   *

In this book, I have argued that a successful anti-austerity strategy must ascend the three vertices of class, state and ideology.

We need a working-class-centred strategy that is not reductive – that neither reduces the working class to its organised layers nor ignores the ways in which it is structured by gender, race and so on. The '99%' is not just an alliance of white male workers, but of every heterogeneous element that is oppressed and exploited and stands to lose from austerity and entrenched neoliberalism. We need trade union action, but we also need to activate many people beyond that; we need a militant social movement.

We need a strategy with regard to the state that is neither statist and parliamentarist nor simply dismissive of the state in an ultra-left fashion. We need to be attentive to both the state's role in social reproduction, and thus the position of public sector employees in austerity battles, and the ways in which parliamentary democracy, from the town council to the legislative chambers, are in fact being encircled and eroded by neoliberalism. Our strategy should involve building up 'resistances' within the state, both among public sector workers and in the parliamentary apparatuses. And at critical moments, it should seek to cause 'ruptures' in the state, to disorganise the power bloc and empower democratic forces beyond the state.

---

45. For some useful background on the effects of different patterns of organising, see 'Why Students in the Rest of Canada Aren't a Homogenous Mass', *Dulce et Decorum*, 8 August 2012, available at www.noraloreto.ca.

We need an approach which takes ideology seriously, and which registers the ways in which slow, long-term ideological struggle shapes the terrain and situates people with respect to emerging battles. This has perhaps been our most serious dereliction thus far, and partially accounts for the short-termism – the constant over-optimism about the latest flash-point of struggle, followed by demoralisation in which only the most hardened activists remain – that leaves us flailing every time. When a majority of workers have never had anything to do with a union, will tell pollsters they never talk about politics, support the most draconian cuts to welfare, and are passive or acquiesce in the face of reactionary policies they don't agree with, there is a deep problem of class subjectivity which cannot be overcome by 'walking it off' or having a 'nice day out' on a demo. We can win victories now, but we have a generation of slow, patient work in front us if we are to fundamentally turn things around.

Index

Compiled by Sue Carlton

Page numbers followed by n refer to notes